KT-425-813

THE HOME SPA
BOOK FOR DOGS

QUARRY

GLOUCESTER MASSACHUSETTS

QUARRY BOOKS

THE HOME SPA
BOOK FOR DOGS

NOSE-TO-TAIL TREATMENTS TO SOOTHE THE SOUL
AND AGE-PROOF YOUR CANINE COMPANION

DR. JENNIFER CERMAK

© 2005 by Quarry Books

All rights reserved. No part of this book may be reproduced in any form without written permission of the copyright owners. All images in this book have been reproduced with the knowledge and prior consent of the artists concerned and no responsibility is accepted by producer, publisher, or printer for any infringement of copyright or otherwise, arising from the contents of this publication. Every effort has been made to ensure that credits accurately comply with information supplied.

First published in the United States of America by
Quarry Books, a member of
Quayside Publishing Group
33 Commercial Street
Gloucester, Massachusetts 01930-5089
Telephone: (978) 282-9590
Fax: (978) 283-2742
www.rockpub.com

Library of Congress Cataloging-in-Publication Data
Cermak, Jennifer.
  The home spa book for dogs : nose to tail treatments to soothe the soul and age-proof your canine companion / Jennifer Cermak.
    p.   cm.
  ISBN 1-59253-173-3 (pbk.)
  1. Dogs—Health—Miscellanea. 2. Spa pools—Health aspects. I. Title.
SF427.C397 2005
636.7'0833—dc22   2005007993
                                                                              CIP

ISBN 1-59253-173-3

10 9 8 7 6 5 4 3 2

The Home Spa Book for Dogs contains a variety of tips, recommendations, and recipes for foods and spa products. While care was taken to give safe recommendations, it is impossible to predict an individual dog's reaction to a recommendation, treatment, handling, training, food, or product. Neither the author, Dr. Jennifer Cermak, nor the publisher, Quayside Publishing Group, accepts liability for any mental, financial, or physical harm that arises from following the advice or techniques or using or consuming the products or foods, mentioned in this book. Readers should consult their veterinarians and use personal judgment when applying the recommendations of this text.

Design: Martin Yeeles, Bob's Your Uncle
Cover Image: Barbara Peacock/Getty Images
Back Cover Image: Nick Ridley
Special thanks to Donna Twichell Roberts for the Ginger Bones recipe on page 101, from *The Good Food Cookbook for Dogs*, © 2004 Quarry Books
Jenn Mason, Artist, page 107
Text on pages 97 and 104 excerpted from *Caring for Your Older Dog*, © 2001 Jean Callahan

Printed in Singapore

Contents

Introduction		8
Chapter 1	**The Home Oasis**	**10**
	Stimulating Your Dog's Senses	10
	The Perfect Bed	12
	Feng Shui for Dogs	16
	A Safe Home	18
	House Hygiene	21
Chapter 2	**A Day at the Spa**	**24**
	Home Spa Schedule	24
	Essentials	28
	Setting the Scene	30
	Pampering How-To	32
	Beauty Recipes	33
	Spa Dog Excursions	34
Chapter 3	**Nose-to-Tail Body Care**	**36**
	The Nose	36
	The Teeth and Gums	38
	The Eyes	40
	The Ears	42
	The Coat	44
	The Paws	50
	The Tail	54
Chapter 4	**The Zen Dog**	**56**
	Stretching and Yoga	56
	Relaxation Techniques	58
	Massage	60
	Knowing Your Dog's Body	62
Chapter 5	**Mental Wellness**	**64**
	Your Dog's Emotions	64
	Improving Communication	66
	Common Behavior Problems and Solutions	70
	Socialization	72

Chapter 6	Fitness	76
	Retreats	76
	Water Therapy	78
	Dog Games and Play	82
	Spa Toys	86
Chapter 7	Good Nutrition	88
	Commercial Feeds	88
	Whole-Foods Menu	90
	Gourmet Meals	92
	Water	94
	Herbs and Supplements	96
	Weight-Control Regimens	102
Chapter 8	Spa Living	106
	Establishing a Routine	106
	Good Habits	108
	A Dog's Calendar for the Seasons	112
	Spa Gifts	114
	Heirlooms	116
	Spa Trends on the Horizon	118
Conclusion		122
Resources		124
Photographer Credits		126
About the Author		127
Acknowledgments		128

Introduction

We love to pamper our dogs. After all, they are truly part of the family. Whether out of love, guilt that we cannot be with them every minute, or a personal sense of style, we dog owners are spending a lot of money on fancy dog foods, massages, and grooming. But have you ever considered giving your beloved pet the all-around spa treatment in your very own home? Wouldn't it be fun to indulge your trusted companion while maintaining or even improving their good manners and health? *The Home Spa Book for Dogs* is the ultimate guide on how to lovingly spoil your pet while keeping his or her best interests in mind. Full of practical advice, fun tips, and clever tricks, you can learn how to lavish your dog with premium attention and, in doing so, improve his overall well-being and deepen the bond of your relationship. *The Home Spa Book for Dogs* is the quintessential how-to book for pampering your pooch.

A few generations ago, when humans lived in a more agricultural society, many dogs had jobs to keep them occupied. Others roamed around the farm all day, ate a variety of leftover people food; dogs lived with a human family, a few other dogs, and a menagerie of farm animals. Today, everything has changed. Many dogs are inactive and overfed and, at the same time, highly regulated, isolated, and banned from most public and commercial buildings. They often have no other animal companions, get very little exercise, and have neither a sport nor a job to keep them stimulated and in partnership with their human companion. Areas for dogs to freely run around in are getting harder to find. Dog owners pay more and more for thirty-minute dog walks, expensive toys, and human-grade, processed dog food. Yet most of what our dogs need, we can provide ourselves in the home. *The Home Spa Book for Dogs* will show you how to create a centered dog through balanced living. You will learn the fundamentals of grooming, fitness, nutrition, play and sport, training, and communication. This book will show you how to thoughtfully care for, teach, and pamper your dog. You will find dog games, tips on training, recipes for spa products, and find out how to get beyond the kindergarten training of "Come," "Sit," and "Stay." Learn a new way to live with your dog that melds old-fashioned, clean living with modern thinking and ingenuity—and oh, yes, a splash of pure indulgence.

Chapter I: The Home Oasis

Stimulating Your Dog's Senses

Dog Spa Style
Take every care at your home spa to make your dog comfortable. Rub down your pooch postbath with a fresh-from-the-dryer towel and appeal to his sense of smell and touch.

Most domesticated dogs endure the same routine day after day, with little variety. Eat, walk, wait, walk, eat, sleep, and repeat. Routine and the development of habits are good things, but too much of the same leads to boredom, frustration, and even destructive behaviors. You can have a big effect on the health and well-being of your dog by considering each of his senses, and determining ways to stimulate and enhance each of them through interactive dog games or exciting outings. These stimulating experiences can be introduced by instituting a monthly home spa day. Over time, once you have seen how your dog responds to various sensory experiences, you may decide to eventually have them become part of your dog's day-to-day routine.

Planning Your First Spa Day

Be creative and choose activities that appeal to all five senses: taste, touch, sight, sound, and smell. Provide a range of pleasant sensory experiences, from walks in a busy city to afternoons by the shore. Make some activities intellectually or physically challenging and others, like a soothing massage, pure pampering. Vary the day's events—take an invigorating hike, followed by a tasty meal. Play challenging, fun games for part of the day, teaching your dog an agility maneuver such as winding through a line of poles. Relax at home with a siesta to the sounds of jazz or classical music, or pick an upbeat tune and dance with your dog. Make your dog's day a special family affair or one between just the two of you as a refuge from your world-weary week. If you cannot dedicate a full day, refer to the checklist on page 11, and devote thirty minutes a day to completing the special activities. Remember, in keeping a living, breathing, thinking creature, you make a commitment to its well-being, and if you honor that commitment, you will get back so much in return.

Revitalize your dog. Go on an excursion to a state park and let your dog dig at tree roots on the lake banks and breathe in the pine-scented air.

Basic Weekly Spa Checklist

Special Outing Visit a park, go to the beach or lake, or take a hike.

Basic Training Practice the basics of "Sit," "Stay," and "Come."

Coat Brushing Do an overall brushing with extra care to remove tangles.

Special Meal Serve a dish such as carrots, brown rice, and ground turkey.

Bath Give a moisturizing cleansing with a favorite shampoo.

Ear Cleaning Add ear cleaning solution to both ears and massage in.

Nail Trimming Cut the nails or take the dog to a groomer who can do this for you.

Massage Rub out those doggy kinks and release tension.

Toothbrushing Brush trouble spots like the canines and back molars.

Dog Game Find an empty playground to romp in.

The Perfect Bed

Choosing the right bed for your pampered pooch is one of the most important health decisions you can make. Yet, like humans, a dog's sleep habits will reflect his personal preferences. What kind of bed does your dog prefer? Is it the minimalist wood-floor bed, the rugged outdoor doghouse, a pillow, a puff, the couch, a crate, your bed, a hand-carved Louis XV reproduction dog bed with French-style cover? Unless you give your dog options in bedding, you will not know what is most comfortable for your pet. Dogs are tough, but they also get sick and age and differ in their needs and preferences. Most dogs do not have full use of the household furniture, so consider giving your dog sleeping options. Leave a firm mattress bed that is large enough for your dog on the floor. Set up a covered crate, providing a safe, draft-free den. Keep the door to a cool tiled room open. Leave a mat and covers in a warm area during the wintertime. Wrap each dog bed in a fresh cotton sheet that you can change easily. Keep your floors clean, and change your dog's linens weekly or more frequently if visibly soiled. Since your dog will follow you around the house, place beds in a few strategic locations—the TV room, in your bedroom (unless you have allergies), and in a safe area of the kitchen. This will prevent your dog from lying on dirty floors or carpeting.

Dream Weaver
Ever catch your dog running or whining in his sleep, legs and nose twitching? What could he be dreaming about? The last exciting squirrel chase perhaps. If you and your dog have a memory of a favorite place, bring the outdoors in by placing, under your dog's sleeping cushion, a small sachet of herbs, flowers, or pine needles from a fun retreat. I like to take rinsed seashells from beach walks and place them near my dog's bed for fond dreamy remembrances. Hopefully, your dog will drift off to sleep dreaming of good times.

Dog Insomnia
If your dog is having trouble sleeping, take him outside to do his business—that may be what's keeping him awake.

So when it comes to beds, what qualities separate the unacceptable from the glorious? The wrong bed is one that is lumpy and hasn't been washed for three months, or one that's too small and sparsely filled with stuffed-animal fluff and a synthetic fabric covering. It is always surprising to see beautifully decorated homes with expensive accoutrements and a pitiful dog bed. The perfect bed is comfortable, clean, supportive, and located in a well-ventilated and temperature-controlled area. A revolution in pet furniture is on the horizon; chic and healthful dog beds will be all the rage. For now, surf the Internet and see what you can find, but splurge on a few well-made beds.

Bad Bed Traits

Too small:
Beds where the dog's extremities fall off the edges. Beds should be large enough so that the dog is completely supported.

Too lumpy:
Beds where the stuffing has compressed or clumped together, causing thickening in some areas and no cushion in others. Beds with supportive foam or batting that is failing should be replaced.

Unprotected:
A bed placed in an unsafe or high-traffic area should be moved to a protected location. Beds next to heavy furniture should be relocated.

Drafty:
A bed should not be near a window, door, or in an uninsulated room. The sleeping environment should be a temperature-controlled area.

Dirty:
Bed linens should be laundered weekly or more often, as needed. To check for cleanliness, do the touch test. If the bed surface feels gritty, change the cover.

Too high to reach or jump from:
To reduce wear and tear on the joints, keep dog bed heights to a near-floor position.

When purchasing a cushion for your pet, think about the details. Make sure the cushion is the correct size and can accommodate your pet's outstretched limbs. It should be made of a comfortable, washable material. Place it in a protected area and not too close to an open fireplace.

Let Sleeping Dogs Lie

Dogs, like humans, exhibit a sleep-wake cycle associated with night and daylight, respectively. Whether due to boredom or natural habit, dogs sleep more than humans sleep but also appear to wake more frequently. Remember: a good dog sleeps best after plenty of exercise.

If Your Dog Sleeps with You

- Get a bigger bed.
- Place a clean sheet over the bed quilt and change the linen weekly.
- Make sure the bed is low enough to the ground for your dog to climb onto and off of safely.

If you look at a herd of puppies nestling down for a nap, you will notice that they vigorously cram themselves against one another. Securing one's spot is accomplished by plopping on top of an unsuspecting littermate and shoving. If you own a large dog and let it sleep on your bed, you may have experienced this behavior in adulthood. Letting your dog sleep with you is a sacrifice. Not only will you disturb one another's sleep, but you will also quickly dirty your bed. If you allow your dog to sleep with you, cover your quilt with a clean, washable sheet. Make sure you and your partner and dog have enough room to sleep soundly without interruption. If not, consider providing sleeping quarters akin to your bed in the room; that is, a bed that is cushioned and firm, ample in size, low to the floor, and accessible.

Feng Shui for Dogs

Feng shui, which literally means "air [or "wind"] and water," is the Chinese art by which, through the precise placement of objects, one creates balance, health, wealth, and harmony. You can incorporate the basic elements of feng shui to create a spalike atmosphere for your dog. The principles of feng shui teach you how to live harmoniously with your environment by recognizing that everything around you is alive, connected, and changing. Through feng shui, one balances the extremes of yin

(feminine) and yang (masculine). Examples of yin characteristics are objects that are cool, dark, ornate, floral, and curved, whereas yang qualities are hot, straight, large, light, or plain. Objects are made into or innately possess different yin and yang qualities. Additionally, one must consider the five elements of earth, metal, fire, water, and wood. These five elements encompass the building blocks of everything in your environment. Like yin and yang, the five elements carry qualities of shape, material, and color and must be optimally balanced to optimize Ch'i. Ch'i, which translated means "cosmic breath," is the invisible energy that circulates as the source of prosperity, health, and harmony. Through the principles of feng shui, you can optimize the flow and accumulation of Ch'i energy in your dog's life. Your dog, who spends most of his time indoors, will benefit from good Ch'i in the home.

Since your best friend spends a lot of time sleeping, his snoozing quarters should have good Ch'i and should be weighted toward yin qualities. Do not place your dog's bed under a window or in a corner where Ch'i can stagnate. There should not be any water elements in the room, since the sound of water can disturb your dog's sleep. Do not place the bed directly across from an open door or at the end of a long corridor where Ch'i can travel too quickly. There should not be any heavy objects above or behind the bed, such as lighting, shelves, or cabinets. Minimize mirrors, which could reflect light and movement and frighten your pet. Avoid using bedding made of synthetic fabrics that distribute negative Ch'i. Use cotton covers instead. Select a bed frame constructed of neutral elements such as wood. Place the dog bed against a solid wall away from any door that could swing open. Consider placing the dog's bed on the opposite side of the house from the active front door or garage to prevent him from being disturbed. Once you have reorganized the bedroom, you can address the rest of your pet's living space to maximize good Ch'i. Apply the teachings of feng shui to enhance your best friend's life and reap the rewards of good health, harmony, and fortune.

Good Backyard Ch'i

Examine your yard for the balanced elements of feng shui. To avoid fast-flowing Ch'i, paths should meander instead of follow a straight line. For the same reason, the back door and garden gate and path should not be aligned. Combine wood, stone, and water—different yin and yang elements—in the garden. Avoid landscaping with sharp corners. Opt for rounded garden designs. Keep the yard free of clutter and animal waste.

Function and Fashion
Good fashion sense means choosing a collar like this lucky dog has: a bright and reflective material to keep the cars away.

I.D. and Tracking
No dog is safe without an identification tag, tattoo, or microchip. If your dog gets out of the yard, is stolen, or runs off during a walk, microchipping or tattooing are permanent ways to identify your lost pet should he or she end up at a shelter.

Poisonous Foods and Plants
Chocolate, grapes, poinsettias, wisteria, daffodils, elephant's ear, azalea, nightshade, and foxglove are a few common culprits that should definitely be avoided. A poisoned dog may vomit, have difficulty standing, drool, have an irritated mouth, have a painful abdominal area, experience a seizure, collapse, or die.

A Safe Home

Safety is the first building block in creating your home oasis. Your best friend has keen instincts but the intellectual capacity of a toddler. Since dogs and humans have lived together for centuries, most accidents are predictable and, therefore, preventable. There are several categories of dangers you must safeguard against. These include poisoning, burns, electrocution and strangulation, choking, and trauma. Protect your dog from accidents in the home; with just a little planning, you can thwart serious injury to your pet and even your family.

Poisons

Poisoning can occur from ingestion of obvious chemicals such as antifreeze or unexpected toxins found in fertilizers and pesticides. Put all chemicals (from paint thinners to bleach) in a place away from your home's living area, ideally the garage. You can put your cleaning products in a small box that you take out only during weekly cleaning. Medications should be kept in a high cabinet and not on a dresser. Think about what an exciting toy a bottle of vitamins is to a dog, as it rolls and rattles across the floor. Your dog could toss it around, then chew through the packaging and ingest the contents. Remember to keep toilet seats lowered, especially if you use bleach tablets. Food known to be poisonous to dogs, such as chocolate, should never be accessible.

Burns

If your dog "surfs" the countertops, he could decide to grab dinner directly from a heated stove. Both burns and scalds can occur from the hot food or tipped-over cooking pots, so keep your dog out of the kitchen with a protective baby gate when you are cooking. Dogs love warm fireplaces and only learn that they are dangerous after a spark hits them. I have a glass-protected fireplace, but I still have to keep my dogs from sleeping in front of it. Remember, treat only a superficial burn at home; anything more than a small, minor burn requires medical attention.

Electrocution and Strangulation

These are real dangers, especially for cord chewers. It may be difficult, but try to keep cords unplugged when not in use. If your dog is a chewer, put your dog in a room where the cords are unplugged and phone cords are not accessible when you leave the house. Consider using a cord winder to keep cords neatly tethered. Look for unexpected dangers too. I once saw a dog get his collar caught on a bathroom cabinet pull. A dog could playfully pull on a cord attached to a hard object. One good tug, and an appliance could come crashing down on an unsuspecting dog.

Choking

Dogs can choke on anything from treats to small toy parts and household knickknacks. Keep the floor clear of stuff—bottle caps, toy soldiers, shoes, and aluminum cans that can be torn to bits. Take a doggy emergency course to learn to give the Heimlich maneuver to a choking dog. Use a trash can with a heavy-duty lid. It is very common for dogs to pull out and eat items that have a food residue, like TV dinner containers. Just like you, your dog can get food poisoning from ingesting rotten food garbage. Also, avoid giving dogs chicken bones and fish bones. Indigestion is extremely uncomfortable for your dog and you and often results in stomach upset, vomiting, and diarrhea. Common treatment for a dog that has vomited includes withholding food for about twelve hours and then introducing a bland diet of rice and cooked ground beef.

Trauma

Trauma can occur if something heavy falls on your dog, or if he cuts himself on a sharp object. Does your dog jump at a glass panel door to greet you? Does the television rock on its stand when your pooch jumps off the bed? Do you keep your razor blade at dog's reach in the shower? These are all potential dangers. The key to safety for your dog is to expect the unexpected and protect against the obvious. Invest in a veterinary handbook and familiarize yourself with its contents.

Emergency Kit for Home and Car

- Alcohol pads
- Aspirin
- Blanket
- Bottled water
- Compressed activated charcoal in case of poisoning
- Cotton balls and applicators
- Diphenhydramine
- First-aid antibiotic ointment
- First-aid tape
- Gauze bandage rolls and pads
- Grooming clippers
- Hydrogen peroxide
- Leash
- Nylon muzzle
- Physician's light
- Plastic and protective gloves (Injured dogs can bite.)
- Rectal thermometer and disposable covers (normal temperature is about 101°F [38°C])
- Saline solution
- Scissors
- Styptic powder to stop bleeding
- Syrup of ipecac
- Tourniquet
- Towel
- Tweezers

Emergency Plan

Don't wait for a real emergency to figure out how to get your dog to an emergency animal hospital. Find the closest twenty-four-hour facility and visit ahead of time to determine the length of transit, confirm the veterinarian's hours, and assess the staff. Keep the hospital's telephone number programmed on your mobile telephone so you can alert personnel to your arrival and start getting medical help. Program a few neighbors' numbers as well so you can drive and get some neighborly help for your dog along the way if needed. Take a class on emergency care so you can deliver doggy CPR and dislodge items immediately if the dog is choking.

Driving in Style

The best way to ensure your dog's safety is to transport your dog in a car, wagon, van, or sport-utility vehicle built to accommodate a dog crate. The dog crate will keep your best friend safe, allow you to drive unobstructed by your four-legged friend, and will keep the rest of your car clean from muddy paws, nail scratches, and punctures. I recommend an easily cleaned rigid plastic or material cargo cover to protect the carpeting and make cleaning quick and easy. If your car is not large enough to accommodate a crate, cover as much of the upholstery as you can. For safety, remove leashes and prong collars during travel. Pull large T-shirts over the front seats, and cover the seats with blankets or towels. Use a hammock-style car protector for the rear seats, with a towel spread out for comfort and absorbency. Stash a water-filled spray bottle and baby wipes to clean dirty paws before your dog enters the vehicle. Clean the interior of the car by vacuuming, dusting, and changing the coverings at least weekly. Keeping your car clean by using washable surfaces will help to keep your pet healthy. Your dog can pick up lots of unhealthy germs on his feet during walks, and it's important that you discourage the transport of those germs from park to car to home.

Natural Cleaners

For all-purpose use, mix one tablespoon of white vinegar and one quart of water in a spray bottle. This solution can be used to clean all nonwood surfaces, including glass, counters, and tile. You can also choose to add a tablespoon of ammonia to the mixture. For dirty jobs, use a scouring pad with abrasive baking soda. The baking soda can also be used as a general-purpose deodorizer. Instead of spraying wood polishes, use paste wax or mineral oil. Use lemon juice or crushed fresh mint leaves to add a heavenly scent.

House Hygiene

You love your dog, but maintaining a clean home is challenging when you live with a pet. You will need to take extra steps to protect and enhance your family's and your dog's health and environment. When you have a dog, plan on cleaning the house from top to bottom at least once a week. Dust, vacuum, mop, put everything in its place, and wash the laundry, including your pet's linens. Here are some suggestions for setting up an easy routine:

• Remember to use diluted cleaning solutions and to minimize the amount of cleaners and scented products you use.

• Keep your pet away from the area you are cleaning so your dog does not breathe in sprayed chemicals.

• For a quick but effective cleanup, dust wood, tiled floors, and furniture with scentless baby wipes or washable damp rags.

• Keep a stash of white cleaning rags that can be laundered and reused. Wipes and rags do a great job of cleaning and picking up dirt while not overwetting surfaces.

• For a gentle cleaning solution, mix a tablespoon of white vinegar in a spray bottle of water. You can also clean glass surfaces and windows with this solution and save money by forgoing expensive cleaning products.

• Vacuum slowly to pick up loose hair, and replace the vacuum bag often to ensure good suction.

• Oil wood furniture as needed. Use washable slipcovers on couches or cover them with sheets or machine-washable cotton blankets. Sheets work well, since they can cover a large surface area and can be washed and dried quickly. If you allow your dog on beds, put a clean flat sheet over every bedspread, and wash the sheet weekly. Remember to cover the dog's beds with sheets, large towels, or a washable bath mat, and wash them weekly as well.

Top Ten Tips for Good House Hygiene

- Buy a good-looking toy box where you can stash the extra playthings.
- Cover sofas, dog beds, and bedspreads with washable flat bed sheets.
- Vacuum twice a week or as needed.
- Keep the water bowl in a tiled room to prevent floor damage, and avoid using a combination food-and-water bowl that allows the kibble to fall into and spoil the water.
- Run an air filter in the room you and your dog use the most.
- When the weather is nice, feed your dog outside to reduce mess from runaway kibble.
- Brush your dog at least weekly outdoors.
- Wash your dog every three months, or more often if smelly.
- Housebreak your dog. Keeping a house clean with repeated accidents is an uphill battle that you will lose.
- Launder linens, towels, and clothes using a hypoallergenic, unscented detergent.

Top Ten Tips for Good Outdoor Hygiene

- Generously spread lime pellets over the grass to neutralize urine odors.
- Pick up your dog's eliminations often.
- Provide an easy-clean bathroom surface like fragrant pine needles, which are easier to pick up and replace then grass mess.
- Remove toy parts, broken glass, and trash from the lawn.
- Keep doggy areas pesticide-free. Release predatory live ladybugs and praying mantis cocoons instead.
- Choose dog-friendly, hardy, and nonpoisonous plants that can withstand abuse and trampling.
- Keep a bowl of fresh water outside. Watch out for decorative ponds that support mosquitoes and parasites.
- Secure the fence; look for any holes or loose boards or wires.
- Make sure your dog has an outdoor safe haven, a covered house away from sun, wind, and rain.
- Correct your dog for destroying tree bark, roots, and bushes, and provide enough toy distractions to keep him playing.

Chapter 2: A Day at the Spa

Dog, Beach, Stick
Finding a dog-friendly beach is a challenge but worth the effort. Take your pet on a seashore excursion. Run, walk, and swim with your dog. Let him dig for the biscuits you have hidden under the sand or chase a stick flowing to and from the shore with each wave. Shake rockweed at your dog for a dirty game of keep-away. Hunt for fish in the shallow waters. Watch your dog wiggle on his back, twisting from side to side.

Let's Go to the Park!
If you don't live within walking distance of a dog-friendly park, get in your car and drive to one. Look for parks set back from the road where there are not a lot of strange dogs. State parks are great. Carry a mobile telephone; wear long sleeves and pants and bug repellent; and pack your car with a first-aid kit, bags for scooping, clean towels, fresh water, you, and your dog. Forget the gym membership; your dog will work out with you for free.

Home Spa Schedule

Reserve a day for your dog at the home spa once a month or, if you have less time, once a season. Notify family members in advance so you can work uninterrupted. A few days prior, you should plan your dog's services, making a list of the products and tools you will need. The content and order of services can vary, but I recommend you always begin a home spa day with a doggy bathroom break, a regular meal and water, followed by fitness and sport. This will allow your dog to hydrate and raise his blood sugar, loosen up, stretch, release tension, and empty his bowels. Many dogs do not get enough time outdoors and succumb to years of boredom, so a morning visit to the park will make the rest of the day flow smoothly. Remember that this is a home spa day for your dog, not for you. I guarantee you will get quite a workout and also plenty dirty. You will save money, and best of all, you will get precious one-on-one time with your pet. You should tailor the schedule to the weather and to your dog's health and fitness needs. Most importantly, keep the day fun and leisurely. Allow your dog time to do the things he enjoys: breaking sticks, sniffing at seemingly nothing. In our hurried lives, we frequently yank our dogs along an obligatory thirty-minute walk and forget to stop and smell the roses, or fire hydrants, as the case may be.

Express Spa

- **Outdoor Excursion with 5-minute Training** (1 hour)
- **Bath and Towel Dry** (15 minutes)
- **Light Meal** (10 minutes)
- **Brush** (10 minutes)
- **Ear Cleaning** (5 minutes)
- **Teeth Brushing** (5 minutes)
- **No-fuss Nail Clipping** (5 minutes)
- **Massage with Siesta** (20 minutes)

Fun in the Sun

Safety around water also applies to pets. Even if your dog is young and active, don't ask your dog to fetch a stick from a tumultuous sea. Your dog could become physically overwhelmed by the surf, current, distance swimming, or water temperature. Have your dog wear a life preserver made for dogs to help him float in dangerous coastal areas or if you take your dog boating. When you return home, rinse your dog clean with fresh water to remove dirt, salt, and sand. Don't forget to clean the toes, as embedded sand can cause nail infections.

Home Spa Schedule

- **"Doing Business" Jaunt** (15 minutes)
- **Breakfast** (15 minutes)

   *For an additional added treat, crack a raw egg over the morning portion of kibble.

Outdoor Excursion with Warm-up Stretch

- **Brushing during Excursion** (5 minutes)
- **Walking, Jogging, Training** (intermittently during excursion)
- **Return Home for Lunch** (15 minutes)

Siesta with Spa Services

- **Massage** (30 minutes)
- **Nail Clipping, Buffing, and Filing with Paw Wrap** (15 minutes)
- **Nap Time** (more than 1 hour)
- **Après-Nap** (30 minutes)
- **Bathroom Break with Brushing** (15 minutes)
- **Ear Cleaning** (5 minutes)
- **Bath and Towel with Blow-dry** (30 minutes)
- **Lounge Around the House** (1 hour)
- **Outdoor Excursion** (1 hour)
- **Dinner** (15 minutes)
- **Bathroom Break with Outdoor Brushing** (15 minutes)
- **Teeth Brushing** (5 minutes)

   Indoor Games and Free Time (remainder of the evening)

   Bedtime with Special Hug Session

Learn from the Pros
To gain some expertise before your first spa day, stay with your dog during a grooming session, and get tips from his groomer. Ask questions and find out about preferred products and techniques.

Favorite Dog Spa Treatments
Massage
Mud therapy
Hydrotherapy
Aromatherapy
Pedicure

Spa White
When preparing for your dog spa guest, ensure that all working surfaces are comfortably padded and covered with clean linens.

Essentials

Depending on your personal level of creativity and effort, your list of essential spa tools and products will vary. Before your dog's home spa day, photocopy the list on page 29 and circle the items you will need. As you set aside or purchase your necessities, cross out each circled item. Spend as much or as little money as you are comfortable parting with. You can create a great home spa kit for dogs on a shoestring budget. A day in advance, clean the rooms you will be using and organize any body products and treats. Read the directions for use on the products you buy. Once your dog's home spa day is over, collect the stable items and tools, and store them in a special container. This will keep your dog's items organized and easy to retrieve for the next home spa day. Remember to clean any grooming tools, and do not pack away any damp items.

Tools
- Nail file
- Nail trimmer or grinder
- Nail brush
- Scissors to trim hair covering eyes
- Comb
- Preferred brush
- Toothbrush
- Collar
- Lead
- Chamois cloth and curry comb for short coats
- First-aid kit

Food and Treats
- Smorgasbord of homemade treats and meals
- Tiny training bites
- Purified water
- Food and water bowls

Towels and Linens
- Washcloths
- Towels
- Cotton flat sheets to cover couches, mats, carpeting, or beds
- Pillow
- Blanket

Miscellaneous
- Cotton balls or pads
- Toys
- Disposable gloves
- Cooking pots, bowls, spoons, masher
- Spray bottle
- Measuring spoons and cups
- Sea sponge
- Filter bags and strainer
- Fresh flowers
- Mood music
- Sachet bags
- Blow dryer

Products
- Dog toothpaste
- Otic ear-cleaning solution
- Hypoallergenic conditioning shampoo
- Edible paw balm
- Baby wipes
- Bug repellent

Essentials for Homemade Products
- Rose petals
- Lavender
- Lemon
- Olive and canola oils
- Baking soda
- Beeswax
- Vodka
- Apple cider vinegar
- Peppermint leaves
- Chamomile flowers
- Eggs
- Aloe vera
- Sea salt
- Vitamin E
- Cornstarch
- Oatmeal
- Parsley
- Cucumber
- Honey
- Favorite extract for toothpaste, such as maple or peppermint
- Witch hazel
- Borax (preservative)

Setting the Scene

You will need to prepare two or three rooms in your house, as well as your vehicle for your dog's home spa day: the bathroom, a spa room, and a sleeping area, which can be combined as part of the spa room if desired. All rooms and the car interior should be immaculate. In the bathroom, position towels, a protective floor covering, and your chosen dog shampoo or rinse along with a toothbrush and dog toothpaste. In the car, cover the bottom of the crate or car seat with a clean, comfortable blanket. Pack treats, water, a bowl, a ball, and required gear for the weather, such as bug repellent or a dog coat. Keep a first-aid kit in the trunk and carry a cell phone and compass if you are charting new territory. In the sleeping room, draw the shades, place a blissful bed in a quiet, protected location, and add a relaxing sachet of lavender. The spa room will house the majority of your tools and products, along with more towels, washcloths, linens, products, and any miscellaneous items. Set the room at a comfortable temperature. You should have enough space to let your dog stretch out while you massage, perform stretching exercises, and groom. If you have carpeting or a hardwood floor, consider placing a clean sheet or cotton blanket on the floor. Remove your shoes to keep the spa surface clean. Have a trash can handy in the room. Select soothing mood music for your spa activities. Steep invigorating peppermint leaves in a cup of hot water for a fresh, light scent. Except for the massage and stretching, work quickly to prevent your dog from becoming impatient. The more active your morning excursion, the more likely your dog will be a lump of afternoon putty.

Warming Touches

Towel, product, and mat warmers are available to keep your dog's spa session cozy. Ear cleaning solutions are much more tolerable when they are slightly warmer than room temperature. Heated mats provide a comforting napping surface.

Popcorn and a Movie

What do you do as a grand finale to your busy spa day? Relax. You deserve it. Pop a bowl of natural popcorn, and enjoy an evening movie. Volley popcorn at your dog during commercial breaks to practice muzzle-eye coordination. Caution: Sharing food may lead to begging.

Pampering How-To

Go over the top pampering your dog on a special home spa day. Fill the dog bowl with fine bottled water. Cook a special meal with favorites like chicken, brown rice, sardines, liver, apples, and bananas. Try serving a detoxifying green juice drink, either store bought or a homemade mix of blended green vegetables. To create a healthy home spa snack, freeze melon cubes and mixed berries. Prepare your dog's retreat carriage with clean, cushiony blankets and a picnic lunch. Invite a doggy friend for the excursion. If you are usually stingy with outdoor playtime, double or triple what you would normally provide. Have an assortment of new toys on hand at home to play with. During cooler weather, cover your dog with a blanket and prop his head on a fluffy pillow. Play your dog a song on the guitar or piano. In my home-based tests, playing recorded music, dogs preferred classical, soundscape, and jazz music over rock. The home spa day is all about pampering your dog, so continually watch your pet's reaction to ensure his needs are met. Limit the amount of scent and products you use and discontinue any procedure or product that makes your pet uncomfortable or causes irritation.

Beauty Recipes

Gorgeous Nails
Forget silly-looking doggy nail polish; give your dog a natural buff. Using a nail brush, clean your dog's nails with a combination of white vinegar and baking soda. Rinse, pat dry, and trim your dog's nails and file the tips. Buff the surface of the nail with a file. Mix a few tablespoons of olive oil with the contents of a vitamin E capsule. Rub the mixture into the nails and wipe off any excess. Finish with a final light buff.

Apple Cider Oily Coat Rinse
To treat an oily, flaky coat, mix 2 tablespoons (30 ml) apple cider vinegar or squeezed lemon juice into 1 quart (0.95 L) warm water. Crack in a raw egg and add 1 tablespoon (15 ml) olive oil. Pour over your dog's coat. Rinse clear with warm water. The dog on page 32 is enjoying a soft towel wrap postshampoo.

Cranberry-Oatmeal Cleansing Wash
As an alternative to heavy soaps, make a batch of gentle cranberry-oatmeal cleansing wash. Boil fresh cranberries in 1 quart (0.95 L) water until they pop open. Spoon out the cranberries, and mix $\frac{1}{2}$ cup (110 g) oatmeal into the remaining liquid. Rinse your dog with fresh water and then apply the cooled cleansing solution to the coat. Rinse clean with warm water. The slightly acidic cranberry water will gently clean the coat while the oatmeal will calm irritated skin and soften the fur. Raw oatmeal shampoos work best on dogs with short coats, as they are easier to rinse out.

Cologne pour Chien
For a light summer scent, pour rose water into a clean spray bottle. While protecting your dog's face, spritz the rose water sparingly over the coat and allow to air-dry. You can make the rose water yourself by boiling fresh-picked organic roses in water. Fragrant tea roses work the best.

Spa Dog Excursions

Mixed-breed, toy, working, herding, terrier, sporting, hound, toy, and nonsporting: nine groups encompass a rainbow of dogs in all shapes, temperaments, and sizes. Try tailoring your home spa excursion based on your dog's breed. If you own a mixed-breed dog, does your dog have a predominant breed characteristic that you can appeal to? The nonsporting group is equally diverse, so take your dog's pick of excursions for a fun-filled day. Here are four different special excursions to choose from that are sure to bring you and any breed of dog fresh air, exercise, and lots of fun.

In-Town Hound

Sight-and-scent hounds love to follow a trail, so plan a city excursion that appeals to their tracking instincts. Certain breeds of sight hounds are built for speed, so you may want to run fast dogs off-leash in a large field before heading to the city. Buy fuzzy chenille sticks from a craft store and ask a friend to put them in his or her laundry bin or other heavily scented location for a day. Place the chenille sticks in a sealed plastic bag until you are ready to use them. For the excursion, go into the city and give the same friend a head start of about thirty minutes, walking and twisting scented chenille sticks every few blocks. The chenille sticks can be placed creatively outdoors, twisted around tree branches, door knobs, sidewalk grates, whatever is in the path of your walking friend. Once you and your dog are ready, show your dog a scented chenille stick and give him a liver treat morsel. Start off in the direction of your friend, letting your dog lead the way, making all of the directional decisions. Reward him for each chenille stick he finds. Watch him as he feverishly works, smelling the ground and air for clues. So you don't get too far off track, carry a mobile telephone to stay in contact with your accomplice. At the end of the tracking session, reward your dog by letting him find his search subject waiting comfortably at an outdoor coffee shop. Relax with two lattes and one bowl of water.

Sporting Dog

These dogs love to run far, very far. They also like to hunt for things. But what do you do when you have an itty-bitty yard and stalking the cat is off-limits? Rent a field for the day and let your dog run amuck. There are trial fields that dog groups rent for hunting events that you can reserve for short money. Pick a day that has not been booked; pack your car with friends, your dog, lounge chairs, towels, dog necessities, and a picnic. Try some surf-and-turf hunting games for fun-filled variety. Bring a buoy you can throw in the water, and let your dog retrieve in a pond.

Summer Fun Run
Did you know that dogs have sweat glands concentrated on the pads of their feet? To cool down in the summer heat after a workout, stand your dog in a baby pool full of cool water and ice.

It's All Good
What part of the spa day does each breed prefer? One hundred percent of all breeds surveyed liked the park excursion best, followed by a savory gourmet meal, and thirdly, the spa massage.

Tear-It-Up Terriers

These plucky dogs are adept at hunting vermin in holes and tunnels. No rat holes on your property to keep your terrier entertained? Unless you actually want your dog to catch a rat, create an artificial, outdoor course of holes and tunnels. You will need the help of a friend with a gerbil or rodent pet and a few household items. Cut an old cotton T-shirt into short strips, balling each strip by tying it in knots. Ask a friend to keep the cotton-strip balls with his or her gerbil for an hour to pick up its scent. Place the balls in a sealed plastic bag until your dog is ready to play. Look around your house and toy store for objects to create your terrier course. In the yard place open, empty duffle bags and a few old pillowcases baited with gerbil-scented balls. Space garden chairs in a path, connecting them with covering flat sheets to create an impromptu tunnel. If you are willing to disrupt your garden, bury one of the balls in the dirt to get your dog sniffing and digging. If you have had a large appliance delivered, cut a dog door in the closed, empty box while leaving a layer of balled-up papers inside along with a tiny piece of bait. Your dog will love routing around in the dark. (You can purchase agility tunnels and equipment for a more professional session.) Place the rodent-scented balls in unusual places such as in a bush or under a flower box. Most of all, encourage your dog's good hunting skills and supervise in case your dog gets stuck.

Winter Workers

What do you do with a dog that is really strong and full of energy? Slow him down by letting him drag you cross-country for miles. The formal name for this activity is *skijoring*. The sport is like dog sledding without Alaska, the sled, and with only one dog. Purchase a skijoring harness for your dog, strap on your cross-country skis, and head for the snow. Bring a friend to encourage your dog to run toward them across a snowy field while you ski behind. If you have never mushed with your dog before, you may spend a lot of time standing still or going fast only sporadically. Run, run, run, STOP, sniff. Unless you jog with your dog, he may not understand, initially, the idea of maintaining a consistent pace. Give lots of praise and work with your dog to hold a speed. Most likely, if you lose your balance and fall down, your dog will stop and wait for you to get up. Isn't that nice? Wear gloves and be prepared to take a fall. Recover by a warm fire with a cup of cocoa. Not up for the snow and skis? Strap on a pair of in-line skates and attach a leash to your dog's body harness. Let him pull you along a paved bike path. You may be pulling him by the end of your excursion, but that's what friends are for. If skijoring or in-line skating are not your style try sledding with your dog —its fun for both of you!

Summer Heat, Sunscreen, and Your Dog

Some breeds when exposed to UV light develop changes on the nose surface that lead to ulceration. A dog with this kind of problem could benefit from sunscreen applied to the nose and being kept indoors during peak sun hours. However, most dogs do not suffer from this condition.

Heatstroke, however, is an emergency medical condition that can fatally affect all breeds. Heat stroke usually occurs when a dog is left in a car or building on a warm day or is outside in hot, humid weather. If your dog appears to be struggling in warm weather, begin cooling him down immediately while you look for a rectal thermometer. Cool your dog in a baby pool full of ice bags, cold water from a hose sprayed over the body, or air-conditioning. A dog with heatstroke might have a rectal temperature of 103°F (39°C) or higher and could die without quick treatment. Once you have brought your dog's temperature down, get to a veterinarian immediately.

Chapter 3: Nose-to-Tail Body Care

A Dog's Garden

When the weather begins to warm, plant a sunny section of the garden with fragrant plants for your dog spa products—different varieties of peppermint, lavender, chamomile, basil, and a tea rose bush. Keep this garden pesticide-free for the safety of your pet.

The Nose Knows

Why not challenge your dog with a game that relies on a keen nose. Rainy days indoors can be livened up with a fun search for hidden liver snacks. Observe the different skills your dog uses: outstretched nose searching for scent in the air, nose to the ground following a trail, reverse sneezes to expel old scents so new ones can be gathered.

The Nose

At home, care of the nose should be limited to observation and the application of sunscreen or protective, lubricating mineral oil or petroleum jelly if required. You should seek professional veterinary attention if the nose is visibly injured or if you see a nasal discharge that is foul smelling or bloody. You should also take your dog to the veterinarian if you see frequent or sudden-onset pawing at the muzzle or sneezing. Your dog may have an allergy or a foreign object in the nose. Keep a physician's penlight in your first-aid kit to better see into the nose, eyes, and ears. Collapsed nostrils are an obvious signal to get to your veterinarian pronto. Other problems include tumors or polyps in the nose, callus of the nose, and infection from a tooth abscess or allergy. Look for any changes in color or texture of the nose, and speak to your veterinarian about how you should care for your pet.

The dog's nose and sense of smell are astounding. Possessing a sense of smell some 100 times greater than ours, this unassuming organ pours information into your dog's brain. A good example of your pooch's miraculous smelling ability is the talent exhibited by cadaver-sniffing water dogs. I had heard of search and rescue, but dogs trained to water rescue are equally inspirational. Where even sonar fails, these dogs have been known to locate wreckage at the bottom of oceans. Heads hanging over the side of a boat, the dogs bark to mark a location. It is believed that they smell tiny gas bubbles breaking at the water's surface. That said, be careful about the heavily scented products you use in your home, especially for cleaning. And do not use aromatherapy products without professional consultation. What smells nice to you could be overwhelming to your pet. (Similarly, what smells attractive to your pet, such as dead fish or rotten food, may not smell good to you!)

The Teeth and Gums

Since dogs do not smile, an unkempt mouth can easily go unnoticed. Sparkling puppy teeth become ringed with shades of yellow and brown, the effect of neglect and gum disease whittling away at teeth and bone and infecting gums. Brushing a dog's teeth daily has not caught on yet as a pet-care must. Designer pet foods have become wildly popular. Visits to the groomer and veterinarian have always been a standard. But toothbrushing regularly has been done by only a handful of dog devotees. Some dogs have their teeth brushed every day; some never. For others, it is once in a lifetime, when professionally scaled by a veterinarian under anesthesia. Think about what would happen if you stopped brushing your teeth altogether. You would get sick from gum infections and inflammation, plaque and calculus would build up, and cavities would abound. You might not see your dog's teeth that often, but out of sight should not be out of mind. To help you remember, make a habit of brushing your dog's teeth at bedtime along with your own, or encourage assistance from your children and pay a quarter for each day they complete their dog's tooth brushing. There are nutritionally based holistic forms of dental care, but I find that nothing beats the classic toothbrush. Your dog is counting on you to keep him healthy through sound dental care.

Toothbrushing 101

Clearly, this experience is easiest if it is started while your dog is a puppy, but all dogs of any age can adapt and benefit. Select a soft-bristled toothbrush sized well for your dog's mouth. You may need to use a children's toothbrush that is not too thick and can reach the back molars.

Put doggy toothpaste on the brush, and press the paste into the bristles. This prevents a dog from eating the icing off the cupcake, so to speak, and losing interest. You can train your dog to enjoy toothbrushing by allowing him to gnaw on a toothpaste-laden brush while you move it around the mouth.

Keep the initial sessions short and fun. Act like you and your dog are playing with a toy. In this initial play-training, you could "eat through" a toothbrush a session, so purchase low-cost brushes. Step up to more focused brushing, being sure to gently brush from the gum line downward. Brush both sides of the hard-to-reach teeth in the very front and very back. Allow your dog breaks to breath, lick, relax, and swallow, even if you don't get this luxury yourself at the dentist. Rinse the toothbrush once you're done and change it every few months or if it becomes damaged.

How to Make Doggy Toothpaste

Add water to baking soda to form a thin paste. Sprinkle in some artificial sweetener. Add one drop of your dog's favorite flavor extract, such as peppermint, maple, or vanilla, or ground cinnamon. You can add a sprinkle of salt for its antiseptic and abrasive qualities.

No Time to Brush?

Shop in the kitchen implements and cleaning aisles for a nontoxic bristled cleaning tool that is a hybrid between a toothbrush and a toilet scrubber. Something that has soft bristles and a plastic handle that is long enough to be steadied between two paws. A back scrubber might work well. Apply some dog toothpaste to the brush and let your dog clean his own teeth. Be sure to take the "toy" away if bristles start falling out or if the plastic handle becomes damaged, and never leave your dog unsupervised with a brush. You can also help keep teeth clean with edible chew toys or those made of plastic, material, or rope. Dogs will spend hours chewing on sheep hooves. Once wet, they will make your house smell like a barn, but maybe you have fond memories of cleaning stalls as a young equestrian. Because of the smell, hooves are great outdoor chew toys. Chewing is a way dogs can ease stress and clean their teeth at the same time.

Lip-Licking Good

In my home taste test, poultry and peanut butter flavors were preferred by dogs 10:1 over mint-flavored toothpaste. Initially purchase a variety of flavors and see which one your own dog prefers. For a no-frills toothpaste, wet tooth-brush bristles and touch the tips to baking soda. Begin brushing as usual. Why should you not use your own toothpaste? Dogs cannot spit and rinse afterward like we do, and the frothing of people tooth-paste is unpleasant to dogs.

Chopper Maintenance

Without proper brushing, dogs get gum disease and tooth decay just like people do.

The Eyes

The Eyes Tell All

Common eye expressions include the heavy-lidded sleepy dog, the wide-eyed panicked dog, the even-set happy or calm dog, and the fixed-gaze aggressive dog.

There is little to do on a home spa day with regard to eye care as these delicate organs should be left untouched unless there is a problem. Use your own eyes to look for signs of illness. Make sure the eyes look clear and that there is no discharge, tearing, tumors, cloudiness, eyelid inflammation, or bulging or sinking. Observe the eyeball surface for any dryness or eyelashes that grow toward the eye. Both eyes should look similar in size and shape. If your dog appears to have any eye pain, go to a veterinarian immediately. How do you know if your dog has eye pain? He may squint, tear, cry, or paw at the eyes and avoid light. If you suspect a vision problem, assess your dog's eyesight. Move your finger toward each eye and see if your dog blinks as your finger moves closer. Test each eye separately.

So, besides looking and assessing, what can you do for the eyes on home spa day? If your dog has long hair about the face, trim it so the hair can't reach the eyes and accidentally scratch the eyeball. That's about it. Eyes are usually maintenance-free. However, remain vigilant as eye injuries or illnesses can become permanent if left untreated.

The Ears

Dog ears are sensitive, and not only in the hearing sense. Unfortunately, they are prone to infections, so keeping them clean is essential. Convenience items are booming for pets and people alike. First came baby wipes, followed by household cleaning wipes and face and hand wipes for an on-the-go refresher. New to hit the shelves are ear wipes for dogs—but don't be fooled, wiping your dog's ears is not always enough. You need to use a liquid ear-cleaning solution to get deep enough into the ear canal to be effective. You can purchase an otic solution at most pet-supply stores or from your veterinarian, or you can make the solution yourself by mixing white vinegar and water in a 1:2 ratio. Regularly inspect your dog's ears for discharge, and sniff for any foul odor; then wipe clean the outer portion of the ear and put a generous amount of ear-cleaning liquid in each ear, followed by a gentle massage. Next comes the unceremonious turning away (akin to running from a wet dog) because what always follows is a rapid headshake, with liquid flying in all directions. (Tip: You might want to do this outdoors.) As a final step, inspect and wipe the ear to remove any further wax and dirt that the liquid has loosened. If your dog is scratching at the ears and flapping away in discomfort because of dirty, moist, infection-ready ears, follow the above ear-cleaning protocol to keep your pet healthy, mite-free, and happy. For persistent or serious problems, take your dog to a veterinarian immediately. Your dog could be suffering from allergies, infection, or mites.

Ear Cleaner Recipe

1 part white vinegar

2 parts water

Some recipes call for the addition of alcohol, which may or may not be irritating. Dogs with sore ears from allergies or infections will probably experience stinging from the solution. Talk to a veterinarian about treating this kind of problem professionally.

Ear-Cleaning Tips

Many dogs dislike liquid ear-cleaning solutions—you probably would too—so work quickly and with a solution that is room temperature or slightly warmer. Test a drop on your own hand to see if it is too cold or too hot. I prefer to use a bottle the size of my palm for two reasons: it keeps the bottle from the dog's sight and allows me to warm the soution.

Hold the dog with one hand while adding the ear solution and massaging the base of the ear opening for a few seconds with the other hand. The massage technique allows for good penetration into the canal and appears more tolerable to dogs.

While any form of dog ear can get dirty or infected, floppy ears in dogs that frequently swim are bastions of dirt and moisture and require extra attention.

The Coat

A beautiful coat is the product of many factors, the most influential of these factors being genetics, nutrition, the seasons, and maintenance in the form of brushing and shampooing. Feel the texture of your dog's coat to help you select the perfect spa shampoo. Using your fingers, spread the fur aside to get a clear look at the skin surface to check for flaking or irritation. Run your hands through the coat, feeling for tangles and dryness. Usually, coats tend to be overly dry rather than overly oily. If the coat feels dry, use a conditioning shampoo, which will keep the hair moisturized and tangle-free. If the coat is oily, you can use a more clarifying shampoo. Use caution, however, as overbathing or use of strong shampoos can strip oils that protect and give shine to the hair. To patch a dry coat, apply a conditioner to fortify and smooth.

Lustrous Locks

Genetics and weather aside, what you feed your dog and how you care for the coat will affect its quality. Some people bathe their dogs far too much, others not enough. I recommend you ask a trusted friend if your dog smells less than rosy; your nose may no longer be attuned to the bad odor. Ask your veterinarian or a groomer to assess your dog's coat quality.

Why Bathe?

Most dogs are given a bath for the following reasons: when they need a haircut and are sent to the groomer's, when they get their summertime flea and tick-retardant shampoo, when they roll in something terrible, when they get "skunked," or when they look or smell dirty. So, if you have decided to give your dog a bath, what should you do and what shampoo products should you use? Let's tackle the first part of the question with a note of caution: A lot of dogs abhor clean, warm bath water. I'm always amazed that ice-cold or filthy, stagnant pond water is far more appealing to many dogs than bath water. In summary, be prepared for bath resistance. How can you prepare? Have the towels, a dipping cup, and shampoo within arm's reach and be prepared to get very wet (wear flip-flops). Outdoor baths with a hose work very well, as do showers or a bathtub that has a hand-held sprayer. What else should you do? Always brush the coat before a bath to avoid getting gobs of loose, wet fur all over your hands (see brushing techniques below). This will also reduce the amount of loose fur that could clog your pipes. If advised by your veterinarian, to avoid irritation, apply a protective ophthalmic ointment to the eyes in case you get soap in your dog's face. You can buy these petrolatum-based sterile gels from pet-supply stores. Put a dry cotton ball in each ear to keep the water at bay. Check that the water is warm—and not too cold or too hot.

The Right Shampoo

Now let's consider shampoo choices. Shampoos for people abound, and pet shampoos are catching up. There are herbal shampoos, scented shampoos; waterless (for those owners who have lost the Bath Battle), medicinal shampoos, tearless shampoos, oatmeal shampoos, tea tree shampoos, and antibacterial, color-enhancing, and hypoallergenic shampoos, to name a few. A lot of these shampoos are very expensive, with flashy claims and advertising: "Richer lather, coconut scent." If you really wanted to use a shampoo with a scent that appealed to your dog, you'd buy Putrid Scent shampoo, with "just-rolled-in-dead-thing aroma." If your dog has a coat or skin problem or has hives or scratches a lot, talk to your veterinarian about what shampoo to buy or be prescribed. Your veterinarian may want to inspect a skin scraping under a microscope to look for mites. If the coat is normal, use a gentle, hypoallergenic shampoo. Yes, it's boring and missing the flowery-fresh smell, but it really is a safe choice for your dog. I also like to use a conditioning shampoo to facilitate brushing and prevent drying. You can use a shampoo sold for people or dogs as long as it works well for your dog's coat type. You do not have to use a tearless shampoo; just keep shampoo off the very top of your dog's head, where it will run with water into your dog's face. Also, place your cupped hand over your dog's forehead as a barrier to keep water out of the eyes when rinsing the head.

Shower Power

Owners with small or older dogs may not encounter much bath resistance. Lucky them. Owners of sporting and working-class dogs, beware! To single-handedly help maneuver a large dog into a shower, use an alternate leash position. Attach a leash to the collar and then wrap the leash loosely under the body **(A)**. Collect the leash over the hips **(B)**. Place your other hand at the base of the leash **(C)**. You will now be able to guide the dog while supporting the rear end. This leash position prevents a dog from pulling out of his collar and gives you control over the hindquarters.

(A)

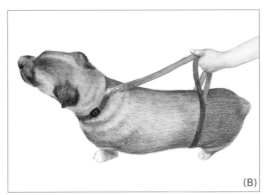

(B)

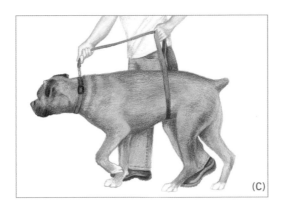

(C)

Outdoor Showering

Want to keep your shower drain working? Bathe your dog outdoors. Using a hose with a nozzle head attached, select a soaker setting, as opposed to a jet setting, which will make you extremely unpopular with your pet. Check the water temperature (initial water from a hose in summer can be too hot) and place a towel and shampoo bottle near where you will be working. (Remember that one hand will be holding the nozzle and the other hand will be holding your dog's lead and rubbing the coat at the same time.) Spread shampoo dots or stripes on a dry coat in strategic areas: chest, neck, hindquarters, back, and so forth. Turn the water on and rinse thoroughly. Make sure you get all the soap off. Gently squeeze excess water from your dog and continue to dry with a towel. Let your dog shake and dry off outdoors if the weather is nice. If you have a long-coated dog prone to tangles, blow-dry and brush the dog to prevent matting. Weather permitting, take your dog outside on a leash and brush out the coat. If you let the "fur fly" outside, you'll do less vacuuming later. As a final step, remove your dog's damp collar and launder it.

The Emergency Waterless Shampoo

Generously sprinkle cornmeal over your dog's coat. Brush to distribute the meal and then continue to brush and shake out to remove excess cornmeal. That's it! A word of caution: This kind of cleaning is recommended only for rare cases when water is not available. For example, I had a dog somehow get a dead rabbit stuck to his collar. The smell left on the dog was tremendous, and there was no water available. Neutralizing the coat with dry cornmeal was a great short-term remedy.

Spa Brushing Techniques

Depending on the length of your dog's coat, you will need an appropriate style of brush or comb. If your dog has a short coat, start with a curry comb and brush in small circles against the direction of the coat to loosen dust and debris. Using a stiff brush, make short flicking motions toward the tail and toward you to pull the dust back and off the coat. Finish with a soft brush across the entire coat and delicate areas, and for a grand finale, wipe the coat down with a chamois cloth. Voilà! For long coats, roll up those shirt sleeves and grab a comb and brush. Ease tangles before combing with a conditioner or detangling spritz. Remember that wet hair is vulnerable to breakage. You can experiment with finding the best brushing tools for your dog. Pin brushes are a good basic tool for long coats, along with a comb. If you have not been brushing regularly, you have a lot of work to do. Honestly though, your dog will be much more patient if you brush for a few sessions during the day as opposed to one long, unpleasant, tangle-ripping ordeal. Tend the coat carefully to avoid ripping and hair breakage. You can use a blow-dryer while brushing but keep in mind that heat-styled hair can lose shine. For an informal look, towel dry a wet coat and then use a pin brush to smooth the damp fur. Comb any tangles free and use a brush to fluff the coat periodically while drying. To maintain lustrous locks, brush all coat types every other day, gently and thoroughly.

For a short-coated dog, start brushing using a curry comb. Brush in circles against the growth of the coat. This will lift debris off the skin. To smooth the coat and remove dirt lifted by the curry comb, use a soft-bristled brush, stroking in the direction of coat growth.

My personal favorite universal brush is the combination pin and bristle brush. One side works great for short coats, and the other is perfect for long.

Combination bristle and pin brush

Slicker brush

Comb

Rake

Curry comb

The Paws

Properly trimmed nails are important to prevent snagging and improper paw placement. However, of all the spa techniques, nail clipping is the most difficult to master. Once a dog has had a painful trim (Et tu, Brutus?), even the sight of a pair of nail clippers can cause anxiety. So much so that owners often give up struggling with their pet and let the nails become unruly. The following technique works well on most dogs, even those that have had unpleasant experiences. Place your dog on your couch and sit next to or in front of him. This will prevent the dog from jumping off the couch and will give you good visualization of the nails. You will need to see what you are doing and have good hand control of the paw to make steady, accurate cuts. Look at the nails and paws to determine their condition. Do this examination before you take out a nail-trimming tool that might send a dog running. Check the paws for cracks, check in between the toes for ticks, and look for any damage to the nails.

To examine your dog's nails and pads, stand shoulder to shoulder and lift one paw backward. Look at the underside of the paw for signs of foot problems. Are any nails split lengthwise or broken off? Is the nail quick, the sensitive inner part of the nail, exposed? Is there visible bruising at the base of the nail? Are there any pad corns, skin warts, thinning, or splits in the paw pads? Are there tears in the webbing between the toes? If you suspect damage from trauma, check for foreign objects such as imbedded glass. If your dog is frequently exposed to hot surfaces or hard pavement that could dry and crack the footpads, the condition could have developed from chronic exposure. Take your dog to your veterinarian for a professional evaluation if needed.

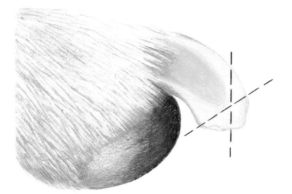

If you trim regularly, as the nail lengthens the outer shell will curve and come to a point in front of the central, sensitive quick. If this is the case, you can cut the tip straight across without causing any pain. Usually the outer shell and quick are aligned, so if you used a cut straight through, even toward the end of the nail, you could cause pain by cutting part of the quick. Remember, if the nails are very long, you will not be able to trim much. You will need to trim sparingly (as in just a few millimeters), but often, to get the nail and quick to regress. When the quick is all the way down to the end of the outer shell, assess the thickness of the shell. Use the trimmers to make 3 short downward but shallow cuts of the external shell area (side, top, and side, akin to grating off a slice of cheese). You will be thinning the very end of the outer nail shell and avoiding the quick. If you feel less confident in your skills, use a hand-held nail grinder. The technique is simpler and is less likely to cause pain, but the noise and vibration can startle an unaccustomed dog.

Start practicing nail clipping early to train your dog as a puppy. However, it's never too late to start. If you encounter insurmountable resistance, begin by rubbing your dog's feet routinely and then move on to filing and then finally to trimming or grinding. Use really good treats to distract your dog's attention during trims. If you cut too close to the quick, you will have to regain your dog's trust. You can also get help from groomers who typically have raised tables with lead attachments. The grooming tables make it easier to see the paws and keep the dog from running away. Stay, help hold and comfort your dog, and ask the groomer to show you what you have been doing wrong in your technique.

Finish nail clipping by lightly filing the nails. Follow with the application of a warm moist towel or mist of water to the paws. Rub a conditioning paw balm into the pads. Create a homemade balm made from edible ingredients and oils such as beeswax and olive oil. (See page 52 for a recipe.) Your dog's spa pedicure is complete!

Pedicure Trim and Tools

You can trim your dog's nails with a nail grinder or traditional trimmer. Guillotine-style tools are available but don't allow you to shave the nail as described here. You have more flexibility when using the two other kinds of tools (grinder or trimmer) and are less likely to cut the quick. Make cuts through the outer shell of the nail and avoid the tender central quick. Only cut directly through the nail if only the shell will be affected. This is generally only possible at the very end of the nail.

Paw Balm Recipe

1 part love

1 part beeswax

1 part olive oil

1 pinch borax

Purchase cosmetic-grade beeswax and follow the manufacturer's instructions for melting the wax. (Beeswax is often sold as a craft supply for making homemade lip balm.) Once the wax begins to cool, begin adding small amounts of olive oil and mix to a thick, whipped consistency, adding a dash of borax. The mixture will continue to thicken as it cools. You can experiment with other edible oils such as avocado oil. Your dog will lick his or her feet once you have applied the balm, so keep your ingredients edible. Store the balm in an airtight container to keep it from drying or discoloring.

Avoid using a paw balm if your dog has very smooth pads, since maintaining a callus is important to protect the feet. Consult your veterinarian if you are unsure about what balm ingredients might be poisonous to your dog.

The Tail

OK, I tricked you. I just wanted to get you near the tail so we could talk about the you know what: the rear end. If you see your dog scooting across the floor or trying to lick his posterior, talk to your veterinarian about having the dog's anal sacs expressed. The anal glands are located on either size of the anus and can be expressed by covering the anus with a cloth while applying external digital pressure using your thumb and index finger. Backed-up anal glands can occur if your dog has soft stools, since passage of firm stools helps to express the glands naturally, as does physical movement. If your dog has loose stools and a gland problem, talk to your veterinarian about changing the diet to harden stools and aid in gland expression. Because of the unpleasant smell and that wary look in your dog's eye, you may find it worthwhile to pay someone else to do this for you. However, once you've learned from a professional, you can perform this technique at home, or better still, outdoors and with a disposable cloth and gloves. Live and learn.

The Family Jewels

If you own an unfixed male dog with a short coat, you may notice that, over the years, his private parts start to look a little chapped. During cold and wet winter months, sitting at every curb takes its toll on the derriere. To rejuvenate forgotten body parts and achieve grooming perfection, dab the skin with a balm or oil such as canola, almond, avocado, or olive.

Location of the Anal Glands

Remember when you learned to hold the car's steering wheel in the two o'clock and ten o'clock hand positions? Well, two and ten are not the location of your dog's anal glands, but five and seven are.

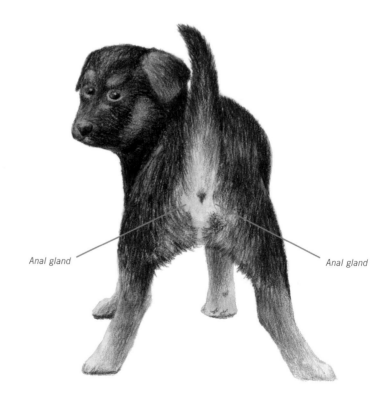

Anal gland

Anal gland

Chapter 4: The Zen Dog

Stretch!

Dogs can be great athletes. Look at the speed and precision of agility dogs or the tireless efforts of police and search-and-rescue canines. Maybe your dog does not participate in an organized sport or job but is equally an athlete when catching a Frisbee or jogging with you. Take a few minutes to warm your dog up, just as you do yourself, before you send Fido racing for a tennis ball.

Stretching and Yoga

Doga, Ruff Yoga, or Doggy Yoga is coming to a city near you, bringing new, literal meaning to the Downward Dog position. If locally available, take your dog for a professionally taught class, learn the basics, and make some friends. While skeptics may think yoga for dogs is over the top, it certainly has a place in the home spa for dogs as well as some fundamental benefits. When you methodically pose with your dog, your dog is relaxing, stretching, and practicing obedience. Maintaining yoga positions takes focus, and learning to hold a position is a novel approach to obedience training. You are not only bonding by working together, but there are also health benefits for both you and your dog. If you cannot find a class or need a guide during your home spa day, rent a yoga video and follow along with your dog as best you both can. Stand over your dog and gently, one by one, lift each front limb forward and each rear limb backward. For another yoga pose, help your dog stand upright on her hind limbs in a Sun Salutation position. Allow your dog to support herself on your arm while standing. While lying down, coax your dog to look at the ceiling, stretching the neck back in a Cobra position. Never overstretch your dog or cause unneeded stress. Doggy Yoga is meant to be tender and calming.

Yoga Blues

As with humans, not all dogs will be inclined to do yoga. Clearly, yoga should be enjoyed by both of you, so if your pooch's reaction is pain and misery, it's probably not his or her bag of bones.

The Downward Dog

Want to impress your friends? Teach your dog the Downward Dog trick. Every leisurely weekend morning, sometime between the bed and front door, your dog might do a backward stretch with his tail in the air and chest stretched to the ground—that's the Downward Dog yoga position. Maybe you can catch your dog doing this after getting up from a slothful evening on the couch. Every time you see your dog do this stretch, say "Boooooowwwwww." When your dog has finished stretching, say, "Good boy (or girl)" as much as you can and run for the nearest treat. Well, that's all you have to do. Just catch your dog in the act a few times, and Fido will be doing encores at your next dinner party. Have fun!

Relaxation Techniques

If your shoulders are hiked up to your ears, you live on processed foods and soda, you endure long commutes, you have financial woes, you have only two weeks a year paid time off, and you have a fifty-plus-hour workweek, chances are you are stressed out. If your dog eats processed dog food, gets a thirty-minute walk a day, lies around alone for hours on end, is overweight, and barely understands "Sit," "Stay," and "Come," chances are your dog is stressed out too. Dogs easily adapt to human schedules, but maybe your schedule and habits are setting the wrong tone. Review the *The Home Spa Book for Dogs* chapters on nutrition, fitness, and communication to learn the building blocks for raising a sound dog. Here are some additional techniques you can use to calm your dog.

Addressing Common Stresses

If your dog has something in particular that he finds stressful, make a special effort to address his angst. Common stresses are visits to the veterinarian and separation anxiety. Take a quick, unplanned visit to the veterinarian's office just to get a treat and say hi to the staff. Have the staff pet and rub your dog. To make departures to work more tolerable, never make an exaggerated event of coming or leaving the house. Set up a daily routine when you leave, leaving lots of interesting toys, the radio playing, and a chew. Consider keeping two dogs together. Ask the dog walker to come at a predictable time each day.

Anxiety Remedy

To help calm a dog in an emergency situation such as a thunderstorm panic, try using calming flower essences. Place a drop of Dr. Bach's Rescue Remedy on your finger and rub it on your dog's gums. This famous remedy contains a preparation of star of Bethlehem (an herb), rock rose, impatiens, cherry plums, and clematis and is a tried-and-true favorite for calming a panicked pet.

Book Smart

Your dog loves the soothing sound of your voice. Sit on your couch or bed with your dog and read a preschool children's book. Make sure the text is simple, one to two sentences per page, and that the pictures are large and clear. Vocabulary books for young children are great choices; your dog will recognize the words he has heard around the house. Another way to impart tranquility is to rub his ears in gentle circular motions. Find the perfect circle size and speed by watching your dog's reaction.

Ten Tips Toward Relaxation

1. Play comforting music such as an instrumental soundscape or classical music.

2. Massage or stroke your dog.

3. Practice stretching techniques with your dog.

4. Go for a long, quiet, unhurried walk.

5. Hug and rock your dog. Holding your dog on your lap, sway forward and back in a rocking chair.

6. Tell your dog what a good boy he is. Repeat frequently.

7. Cover your dog's crate when he sleeps.

8. Sing to your dog.

9. Give your dog a tasty chew to gnaw on.

10. Play a backyard game of fetch.

How to Enjoy Leisurly Weekend Mornings

Roll out of bed. Fill a travel mug full of your favorite beverage or take your dog to pick up some fancy hot beverage at a local coffee shop. Buy yourself a warm, flaky croissant. Three bites for you, one for your dog. Walk with your dog around town until your mug is empty. Visit dog-friendly shops with clerks that give out free biscuits at the counter. Make sure your dog earns each treat by performing a trick or command. Do a little shopping while people coo at your adorable dog.

Heaven Scent

Use limited amounts of natural scents known for their relaxing properties. To release the perfume, crush or cut up fresh peppermint, lavender, or lemon balm. Place the leaves or flowers in a bowl on a desk. Open a window so a gentle breeze can circulate the scent through the room and into the house. You can also steep an herbal teabag in hot water for a subtle, calming scent. Remember that your dog's sense of smell is far more acute than your own, so less is more when it comes to the use of scent in the home.

Massage

No home spa day is complete without a doggy massage. Take your masseuse job seriously and prepare a quiet work area with a bed or thick mat that is comfortable for you and your dog. Perhaps a towel-covered couch will do. Have a clock or watch handy to keep time (fifteen to thirty minutes of massage is a great goal), and play some pleasant music. Make sure your dog is ready for sleep and has emptied his bowels. Place your dog sitting on the massage surface and begin by petting him until he lies down willingly. Progress from stroking to light and gentle massage movements. Hand techniques may include kneading, stroking, raking, light pummeling, pinching, circular movements, gliding, or applying point pressure or holds. Massaging your dog is an experiment, so you will have to read your dog's reactions to your techniques; be cautious, and adjust accordingly. Avoid applying too much pressure to unprotected organ areas like the stomach, throat, near or on the eyes, on joints, and on bony promi-nences, and assess any current medical contraindications like open wounds, scar tissue, or breathing problems. Massage all sides evenly and, most importantly, rhythmically. Your dog should experience blended waves of massage, not intermittent goosing. Be sure to support any suspended limbs with your hand. Use the massage for light stretching and to unfreeze arthritic joints. Utilize a warm mat if that is comforting to your dog. Speak to your dog and tell him what a good boy he is. And he has been a very good boy. You will be repaying him for working late and leaving the park early. A massage postpark is perfect. You can lull your dog into a deep state of relaxation and follow with an afternoon nap for two. Warning: Significant others may become jealous and demand their own massage.

Use the massage as a time postexercise to assess your dog's health. Look for any lame areas, lumps and swelling, cuts, rashes, and ticks. Determine if the ears need cleaning and if the nails need trimming. Check for any weight gain or lack of body symmetry that can result from muscle weakness. Another use of massage is to reward an accomplishment. For example, if your dog hates bath time, follow each dreaded bath with a massage in a sunny spot. Massage can be useful to help trim a dog's nails. If you know how to painlessly cut nails, you can clip them one by one during the massage, and he won't even notice.

Blissful Buttons

Hire an animal acupuncture or acupressure specialist to provide a spa day house call. You can ask the specialist to visit in the afternoon when your dog has completed his morning retreat. You can learn from a pro about any observed trouble spots on your dog before you start your massage. Depending where you live, it may be difficult to find a person qualified to perform dog acupuncture or acupressure. Speak with a holistic veterinarian or conduct an Internet search to locate your local dog resources.

With respect to massage, the anatomical differences between humans and canines are obvious. However, once you get started, you quickly learn another big difference. It's tough to massage around all that hair. Most people are fairly smooth and even smoother with the appli-cation of massage oil. Depending on the coat type, you cannot apply the same gliding motions on dogs as you can on people. Also, the scale is much smaller on a dog with very little flesh around the limbs. But interestingly, the result is the same: massage turns both humans and dogs into happy lumps.

Everyone knows that dogs love to be touched. Petting and stroking a dog is a crucial part of the human-animal relationship. But most petting centers around the head and shoulder regions. Some people take a rough approach to petting, literally slapping the dog on the back or ruffling its fur. Massage approaches touching in a gentler, more mindful way. Dogs love the extended contact and people who massage their dogs find that it relaxes both the dog and them.

Begin by thinking about what parts of her body your dog most likes to have touched. Find a comfortable place on a carpeted floor. With your dog in a seated position, begin at the head, gently massaging the eyelids, muzzle, and nose. From there, work down the neck to the chest and pectoral muscles. Use long, firm strokes. Your dog may offer her paw. You can accept it, but gently put it down again if your dog losses her balance.

The dog may lie down so that her belly can be stroked. Don't forget to massage your dog's legs, too.

Massage can help dogs who are recovering from injuries or fractures get well more quickly. It can also help to restore muscle tone and help calm a stressed dog. Use your intuition and follow your dog's communications about what she likes and dislikes. Try to keep the stroking firm and methodical so that your dog comes to know the difference between getting a massage and just being petted.

10-Minute Standing Dog Massage

Start by stroking your dog down the length of his body. Progress to kneading and rolling movements over the same area, working from front to back. Don't forget to stroke under the chest, not just the top and sides. Facing the front of your dog, run your hands down the back and sides of the neck. Gently rub his cheeks and forehead. Rub under the ears with slow circular motions. Massage each front leg down to the foot, using small, gentle kneads down the leg. Facing the back of your dog, massage the derriere muscles, using two hands to rub each thigh. Warning: The thigh rub is a massage favorite and usually results in a dog lying down in relaxation. I learned it was the preferred massage area when my dog started pointing his back end toward me, while looking over his shoulder at me.

Knowing Your Dog's Body

Posture Perfect

Compare the symmetry of your dog's muscles from one side of the body to the other. When your dog runs toward you, watch if the legs and body follow a straight path. Observe your dog's top line (that's the top of your dog's spine as it runs down the back). If you notice any problems, your dog may be in need of a body tune-up.

Your dog's body structure is built from bones and muscles with tendons and ligaments holding everything together. Starting tip to tail, your dog's skull is attached to cervical vertebrae, which extend to the scapula, which make up what we call the shoulder. The scapula connects to the long bones of the front legs—the humerus and radius, with the elbow in between—and the radius connects to the lower carpals and metacarpals of the paw (akin to the human wrist and hand). The thoracic and lumbar vertebrae (like our spine and lower back, respectively) make up the top line of the dog, with the ribs extending downward from the thoracic vertebrae. The vertebrae continue on to form the tail. The pelvis is attached to the long bones of the hind limbs, with the knee connected to the lower tibia and fibula. Finally, the ankle bones are connected to the tarsus and metatarsals, which round out the feet. Muscles and nerves provide the machinery for movement of the body and organs, with the circulatory system transporting oxygen from the lungs, nutrients, and cellular goods throughout. The skin and coat provide the outermost defense system, with a cellular arsenal within for inner support against bacteria and viruses. The brain allows your dog to interpret information from sensory organs that filter information from the world around him. Most owners are intimately familiar with their dog's digestive and excretory systems, which are supported by a fleet of organs. Last but not least, dogs have reproductive organs supported by hormones that keep them busily interested in one another.

The point of this crash course in dog anatomy is to reinforce that your dog's body is as complicated as your own. Caring for your dog's physical and emotional needs is a necessity and not a fad. You are not spoiling or humanizing a dog by providing healthcare, clean living, wholesome food and fresh water, socialization, and fitness. Dogs kept as pets are deserving of these fundamental elements.

Anatomy of a Dog

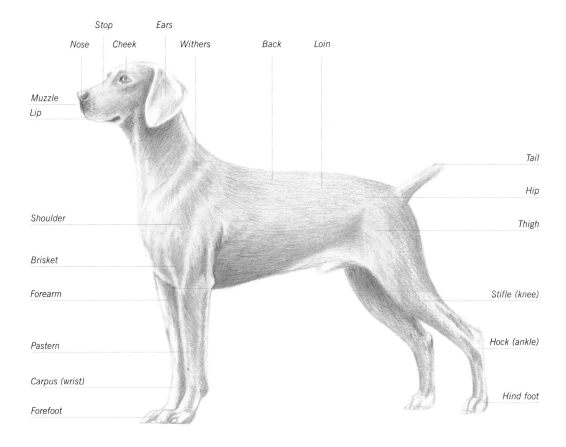

Stop

Ears

Nose

Cheek

Withers

Back

Loin

Muzzle

Lip

Tail

Hip

Shoulder

Thigh

Brisket

Forearm

Stifle (knee)

Pastern

Hock (ankle)

Carpus (wrist)

Hind foot

Forefoot

Chapter 5: Mental Wellness

Wrapped Around His Little Paw

Dogs are really bright. While I was eating my dinner, my dog would suddenly and convincingly become rigidly alert, bark aggressively, and bolt for the front door. Since he was great warning me about visitors, I would leave my plate and walk to the door. It took me a few meals to realize that he was backtracking and stealing food from the table with this diversion. Every time I went to the door, no one was there. He's a smart cookie.

Doggy Etiquette

Does your dog lack manners? Sometimes it is hard to watch your dog get corrected by other dogs. You do not want to see him get hurt. But maybe your dog is rude, not respectful of the pack hierarchy, pushing or shoving, getting in the face of other dogs, stepping on a resting dog, or rough-housing. Only interfere when you believe your dog is really getting injured. Some altercations sound terrible but are physically harmless. Dogs live very orderly, clean lives, and you must trust them to govern their own kind.

Your Dog's Emotions

A centered dog is learned, fit, nourished, watered, and loved. A balanced day for a dog can be broken up into 12 hours of sleep (8 at night and 4 napping), 2 hours of exercise, 1 hour of potty outings and quiet yard exploration, 30 minutes of eating, 2.5 hours of indoor unsupervised playing, 4 hours of following the family around, and 2 hours of active love and affection and training. Your dog should be very happy with this kind of schedule.

Are you Bowwow-lingual-able to talk dog? Dogs are very expressive creatures and use their eyes, mouth, body, ears, and sounds to tell you what they're thinking. Following is a list of basic emotions with their associated canine behaviors. Pay attention to your dog's body language to understand what he is trying to tell you. By learning dogspeak, you will be able to better respond to your pet. This will make him more balanced and centered and will reduce his frustration. You will also learn to interpret the intentions of a stranger's dog. Is the dog friendly or about to bite? By talking dog, you can watch for the telltale warning signs of an impending scuffle. Remember that a dog may not use every aspect of a posture or sound every time. Look for one or two clues that are suggestive of the full pattern of a mood.

An emotion most owners will encounter is whining or frustration over not enough park time or too much alone time. Remember, in general, two hours of vigorous outdoor playtime is enough to meet the needs of an active dog. Your dog is very patient, but even patient creatures have limits. Even when your dog appears content lying around, just pick up the leash and watch how quickly he wakes up and heads for the door.

Common Dog Phrases and English Translation

"I'm shy and will let you be in charge."
Ears pulled against head, tail between the legs, one front foot pulled off of the floor, rolled over on back, whimpering, lips pulled back, licking other dog's muzzle or your face.

"I'm fearful and will bite, because I am scared."
Frozen body. Cowering or lowered head. Growling or baring teeth.

"Will you play with me?"
Dog bows and possibly yaps or barks and growls. Tail wagging. Face relaxed with eyes open. Ears out to sides or relaxed. Jumps or runs near other dogs to encourage play.

"I am a bully."
Dog stands tall, stares, and does not avert gaze. Approaches in a straight trajectory and, with or without further warning, attacks. Growling may not begin until attack ensues.

"I'm top dog."
Dog stands tall with hackles raised and throws head over the neck of other dog. Ears pulled close to head. Bumps or forcefully rolls other dog with body. Pushes in front of other dog through doorways and on stairs. Blocks path of other dog. Gives forceful corrections. Eats first and enforces food privileges.

"What's that noise?"
Dog stands tall. Ears fanned out. Eyes wide. Tail up. Silence or muffled barks followed by load barking.

The Underdog

Occasionally, I have seen a dog ganged-up on at the dog park. One aggressive dog rolls and torments a dog relentlessly until the lesser pooch is immobilized on his back. Then all of the bystanders start to get in on the action and take unforgiving nips at the belly-up dog. If you see this happening, assert yourself as the alpha dog and come to the poor creature's rescue. Disperse the pack, and get the underdog back on his feet. Contain the ringleader.

The Under the Weather Dog

Look for signs that your dog is under the weather. Dogs do not want to show weakness, so clues may be subtle: lethargy, lack of appetite, and being overly quiet. When in doubt, be on the safe side, and examine your dog for any painful areas, distended stomach, injuries, running nose, diarrhea, or vomiting. A great tool you can use is a digital rectal thermometer to check for fever.

Improving Communication

You can teach your dog more than you think. That is to say, you are probably underestimating how smart your dog is and how much more he can learn from you. Some dogs master hundreds of words and commands while others barely learn "Sit," "Stay," and "Come" or pretend they don't know these commands when they really do. Now whose fault is that? Hmmmm? Sharing a common language through sounds and hand signals enhances your life with your four-legged friend and opens a world of possibilities for your experiences together.

The trick to building a common vocabulary between you and your dog is obeying four rules: Consistency, Repetition, Linking learned vocabulary words, and Praise. Consistency means that everyone in the family uses one word for the same command, never uses two words for the same thing, and does not use two words when one is sufficient. For example, use "off" to ask the dog to get down from the couch, and "down" when you want the dog to lie down. There is no need to say "get down" or "get off" when one word is sufficient.

Repetition means that one should practice the vocabulary daily, in short intervals. You can write each vocabulary word on a small piece of paper and carry the words and tiny liver treats in a small pocket-sized case. One word, one treat. Walk with your dog in a park and teach or practice the word on each paper you pull at random from the case. This will help you remember all the words and in different sequences. Start with three words, then five, ten, twenty, and finally the golden thirty (see list on page 69). Think about teaching your dog different categories of words: words for different actions or movements, and names of objects, people, and places. The thirty words on page 69 are very functional and can be eventually linked with nouns and together for further functionality. For example, if you want your dog to bring in his toys from outside, link vocabulary words to give him this command. Tell your dog, "Toy, Fetch, In." When he has picked up all the toys except for one, the one he can't see but you can, say, "Toy, Find" and then, "There" when he's near it. "There" means the object is underfoot, and the dog knows to narrow his search area. Teach as much as you can in play and passively. When your dog jumps on something, say, "Hop." When he's barking, say, "Speak." Talk to your dog, and he will outlearn his neighbors.

see list on page 69

Training Tips

It is easy to train even the largest dog if you remember the golden rule of dog training: Say a command once, only once (he heard you the first time), and always be able to enforce a command when your dog is learning. For example, do not ask a dog to come when, if he does not listen, you have no way of pulling the dog toward you on a lead. Do not set up the situation so your dog is likely to fail at your command (e.g., don't ask your dog to needlessly come to you when he is playing with another dog and you have no reward or control). Remember to praise, praise, praise, and practice in short intervals daily.

Dogs learn and remember hand commands faster and better than spoken words. While it is inconvenient to have your dog look at you for all commands, use both a spoken and a visual signal to help your dog learn. Remember that dogs do not have the best eyesight, so select hand commands that are not complicated.

Basic Commands

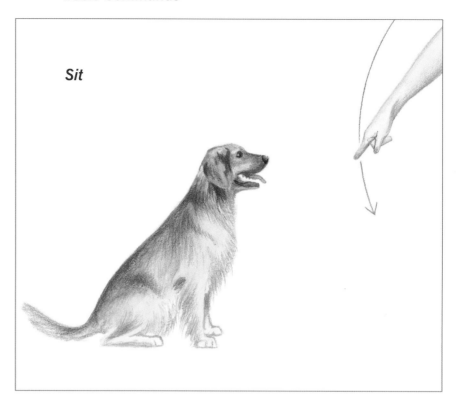

Sit

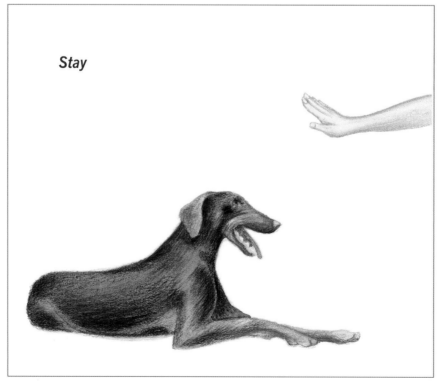

Stay

Down

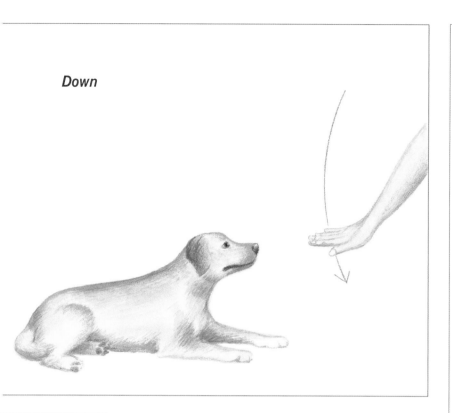

Come

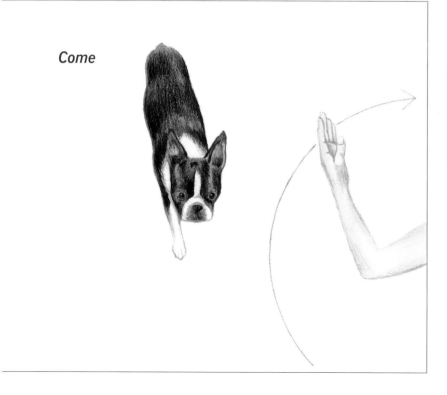

Additional Commands

Heel

Out *(leave the room)*

Hop *(jump onto something)*

Take *(grab object with mouth and hold)*

In *(enter room or house)*

Find

Speak

Drop

Stand

Under

Over

Bring

There *(indicating an object is near the dog)*

Quick

Fetch

Pull

Push

That way

OK *(universal release command)*

Do your business

Slow

Sleep

Shush

Alert/Show *(related to search command)*

Off *(jump off of something)*

Back *(back up)*

No

Common Behavior Problems and Solutions

Is your dog underutilized and without a job? Few dogs can live a lifetime as an unchallenged pet. Left to their own devices, your dog may just take up a job around the house. Most dogs do not get a higher education and, therefore, choose the same instinctual work using natural talents like barking, eating, chewing, begging, and fighting. Following is a list of common careers that dogs pursue and ways you can help them give their notice. Having goals, careers, and challenges are as healthy for dogs as they are for humans. Keeping mentally and physically challenged and feeling needed are important to health and longevity. Give your dog a job: fetching the newspaper, picking laundry or toys up off of the floor and putting them into a basket, finding your lost keys in the house.

Security Guard (barking):
Squirt gun, Hush command with reward treat (keeps the mouth too busy eating to bark).

Professional Greeter (jumping on people):
Practice four-on-the-floor for all petting. Warn guests ahead of time to be firm with your dog if he jumps. Raise your knee up as your dog starts to jump to dissuade him. Practice having your dog sit at the front door while you ring the doorbell. Increase the level of difficulty by having visitors enter while your dog remains seated. Reward good behavior.

Pan Handler (begging):
Never give table scraps at the table. After you have finished eating, put a morsel of food in the dog food bowl. If your dog begs while you are eating, growl at your dog à la alpha chien.

Wood Refinisher/Demolition Man (chewing on the furniture):
Spray bitter apple on tasty-looking furniture corners. Place plenty of toys on the floor to distract him. Correct your dog if you catch him in the act of nibbling the Biedermeier furniture.

Debate Champion (talking back):
Seek professional help because asserting yourself suddenly with an aggressive dog may result in injury (to you). Talk to an expert about ways to regain control.

Bully (biting):
Same as above. Work with a professional dog behaviorist.

Professional Wrestler (roughhousing):
Send your dog outside to burn off the excess energy. Play a game of fetch or give him a toy to play with. For inappropriate racing indoors, block the running dog with a quick "Slow" command.

Shoplifter (stealing food):
Make a habit of keeping paws off the counters and tables. Keep the kitchen off-limits to Fido. Use correction or a squirt gun. Only feed the dog from his bowl. Set up the repeat offender by sprinkling hot sauce over an abandoned plate of food. Do this if your dog is a perfect gentleman when you are watching but reverts to shoplifting when you leave the room.

Garbage Man (trash looter):
Use a trash can with a lid. Employ correction or a squirt gun. Throw a loud rattle near the trash can as your dog approaches it.

Couch Potato (furniture lounger):
Place a comfortable mattresslike cushion on the floor for your dog. Praise your dog for resting on his designated mat. When your dog is sitting on his cushion, go over to him and pet him. For repeat offenders, keep a squirt gun near off-limits furniture as a visual deterrent.

Globe-trotter (runs away from home):
Do not leave the dog unattended outside. Inspect the yard for barrier defects. Consider perimeter training. Make sure your dog has proper identification. Keep the dog busy with a dog sport, excursions, and plenty of playtime. Find fun ways to practice "Come" to entice your dog to respond to your call.

Socialization

Dogs are pack animals by nature, and like wolves, they live in ordered groups. Wild dogs grow up together and are well socialized to kin of all ages and temperaments. The modern pet dog lives a sheltered life with sometimes neither daily interaction with another dog nor, aside from walks, contact with the outside world. Early continued exposure to other dogs, unusual places, and strangers will help your pet become a confident, well-adjusted adult.

Other Dogs

For health reasons, puppies should not be exposed to dogs that may lack vaccinations or be aggressive toward a puppy. Let your dog play under your supervision with a few adult dogs, ones that you know are gentle with puppies and current with their vaccinations. Offer to watch a friend's dog for the weekend so your puppy can spend time living and learning from an adult dog. Invite a doggy friend over for a slumber party, giving your neighbors a chance to send their dog away kennel-free. Interaction with other dogs can be a good thing. Older dogs can teach teenagers and puppies about polite canine behavior. Just be careful that a dog doesn't hurt your puppy, and always watch what is going on.

Noise

If you live in a quiet home, expose your dog to different startling sounds. This will help keep him from becoming skittish. Bring your dog to soccer games with clapping and roaring, to playgrounds where kids yell and squeal, and to the garage while your car is getting inspected. If your dog is nervous about noises, make a big noise when he is eating. For example, drop your keys on the floor, put down the bowl of food, and walk away to let your dog eat. This will link the unpleasant sound to a pleasant event, lessening in time any negative associations. Your dog will learn that sounds in themselves are no big deal.

Children

Because of their size and behavior, children can be at risk around certain dogs. For example, a child holding a piece of food low to the ground could get knocked down by a dog stealing an easy-access snack. A dog could misinterpret a small child's running away and shrieking as play. As we have all seen, children can hurt dogs—pulling ears and tails and slapping or playing horsey. A dog could nip at an offending hand. Listen well: Never hit your dog. If your dog is fearful of hands, he could react by biting a child's flailing arms. Most importantly, always supervise children and dogs. Socialize your dog to children who have some experience with dogs and understand how to behave.

Puppy Love

It is a good idea to limit your developing puppy's exposure to strangers' adult dogs. Puppies get a measure of immunity from their mother. Once separated from nurse milk, a puppy's immunity will wane until he is able, in time, to build up his own acquired immune system. You may be inclined to let your dog greet lots of dogs or take your new pet to a busy pet store to buy basic items. Keep the germs away by keeping your puppy away from strangers' dogs. Let your dog meet adult dogs, but if you live in a city, don't stop and have your puppy meet every dog you walk past.

Busy Areas

If you live in suburbia and leave your dog at home a lot, a busy locale will be a rewarding challenge. Once you've taught some basic obedience commands and learned to parallel park in small spaces, head with your dog to the busy city. Where allowed, shop with your dog in stores to practice a close heel around merchandise racks and walking on escalators. Soon your dog will be able to calmly wait for you in the shoe department while you take advantage of a sale. Your handsome dog will be kept busy with adoring shoppers, giving you a head start on the sale. On your first city walk, practice the commands "Sit," "Stay," and "Heel." Mastering those three words will be enough of a challenge. Walk briskly so your dog has to keep up with you and has to pay attention for your quick halts at street corners. Praise your dog constantly and speak in a calming voice. Tell your dog to sit and let strangers pet him. He will learn that people are nice, and the city is fun. Practice an extended stay outside a coffee shop. The bustle of people with food, other dogs tethered nearby, and the opening and closing of doors will be a good lesson on restraint.

The benefits of varied socialization are numerous and include increased confidence, development of a steady temperament, and the ability to manage diverse situations. Socialization is the foundation to creating a centered pet.

Love Buds

Give your dog supervised experiences with other dogs and animals, loud noises, busy areas, and children. The dog and cat shown here are best buddies and have learned to live harmoniously together.

Tough Love

Proper, quick correction should always be outweighed by praise. Dogs learn not only by discipline, but also by understanding from you what is good behavior. Your dog will endeavor to hear your praises and will avoid any reprimand.

How to Integrate Dogs If One Is Unfriendly

Advisory: Seek professional help if your dog has a history of biting people or dogs. This lesson is not for dogs that have already proven to be dangerous. Here are some tips for introducing two dogs for the first time, if one of them is not so friendly. You will need two people, two leashes, a squirt gun, and a fence or baby gate. If possible, introduce both dogs in a new outdoor environment where neither dog can claim the area as current territory, and a dog can flee safely if attacked. Make sure both dogs have been well exercised in advance and start with a thirty-second obedience routine to set the scene and let them know that you are in charge. Have the dogs meet through a protected shield like a chain-link fence. Reprimand any dog that growls with a sharp "no" and a water squirt, followed by praise for sniffing nicely. If all growling stops, have the dogs meet, both on leash, so they can be pulled away from each other if a problem arises. Praise both dogs by name liberally during the introduction. I recommend you keep the leashes loose, so the dogs do not become tense due to your pulling. Keep the squirt gun out as a visual reminder. Let the dogs sniff noses and rear ends. If all seems fine, let both dogs walk around and continue to greet. Let go of the leash but keep it attached so you can grab the leash without getting your hands in the way of a dogfight.

The same routine applies at home, but with a baby gate instead of a fence. Additionally, you should put away all toys, food, and treats so there is nothing to fight over. If you see the dogs standing tall, throwing their head over the other's neck, humping, growling, or raising the hair on the back of their neck, thwart a potential incident with a reprimand or escalate to the squirt gun. Praise them at all other times to keep them calm, and distract them when they seem irritated, by asking them to come to you for a quick scratch.

Remember, you are the alpha dog. The aggressive dog is not permitted to overly dominate another dog without your approval. Here's another tip: make sure both dogs have urinated prior to seeing each other. If there's a chance a dog might relieve himself out of fear or in marking an indoor territory, you will be glad you did a bathroom stop in advance.

Chapter 6: Fitness

Retreats

Every now and then, load your dog in the car and go on a special retreat. Take a break from the ho-hum regularity of daily walks to visit a place where there are new sights, sounds, and scents to be explored. Getting out of the house will make your dog more travel-friendly and allow you to spend more of your free time with your best friend. Remember that the better trained and groomed your dog is, the more likely you will be to gain entrance into different venues. Use the weather to your advantage by going off-season, during nonpeak times, or in colder or wet weather to avoid the masses. Here are the top ten places to take your dog and the best reasons for going.

Pet-Friendly Hotels
Three cheers for hotels that permit doggy guests! You may find slim pickings, but for a family vacation that's all-inclusive (i.e., includes your dog, too), start by choosing a hotel that appeals to the humans in the group. Next, call the hotel to confirm the cost and discuss restrictions and permission for visiting dogs. Ask about any special services such as hotel dog walking. Last, be sure to prepare a doggy travel case with extra linens, leashes, towels, bowls, food, and toys.

Top Ten Doggy Destinations

1. **Seashore with beach or boardwalk**
   Sand crabs to chase, seaweed to toss

2. **Mountains**
   Long hikes and fresh air

3. **Forest with lake**
   Swimming and sticks are everywhere

4. **Playground, tennis court, or skateboard arena**
   A city dog's oasis from the dog park

5. **Quaint town center**
   People stop and say hello with a nice pat

6. **Farm with fields and animals**
   Other four-legged friends

7. **Neighbor's pool**
   Belly flops in the water, and kids to play with

8. **Pumpkin patch or Christmas-tree farm**
   A nice walk outside with the family

9. **Ski house**
   Fetching snowballs is fun

10. **Big city**
    Fire hydrants are everywhere

Water Therapy

High-Tech Tanks
Taking their cue from the
treatment of expensive
race horses, some dog
therapy facilities have
water tanks with built-in
treadmills. If your dog is fit
and active, go low-tech by
having your dog retrieve a
ball from a lake.

If your jock dog overdid it in the dog park or your pooch is twenty pounds too heavy and hobbles around the house, go swimming. There are months of good weather you can use to your pet's advantage. Lakes are ideal, with their paw-friendly beaches and soft mud bottoms. To encourage your dog to paddle around calmly, put on your swimsuit and foot jellies and get in with him. Put a dog life vest on your dog if you think he may sink and not swim. Start slowly and hold your dog during rest breaks. If your dog is in need of professional medical rehabilitation or you lack the water resources, consider indoor water therapy to speed a healthy recovery from surgery. The water provides buoyancy to help support your dog while stretching and building muscle. Water reduces the wear and tear on joints and foot pads and provides resistance not encountered while walking or running. You can hire a specialist to assist your dog, providing encouraging words and physical support and direction. Arthritic dogs can get into a vicious cycle, adding weight because land walking is painful, the added weight aggravating the arthritis. A few months of therapy to reduce the weight can put your dog's health back on track.

Lone Wolf Howl

Ever lose your dog off-leash? Despite good training, sometimes certain distractions are insurmountable. While walking one day, a huge stag ran full speed across our path. My dog followed and disappeared for what seemed like forever. He eventually came back exhausted and muddy but excited about his recent fun run. If your dog has run out of sight and is not responding to "Come," try calling back your pack. Stay in the spot where your dog last left you and howl like a lone wolf. This is the universal call for wolves searching for their pack members. It has worked for me, and in an emergency, it could work for you too.

Swim Safely

You may encounter a few of mother nature's surprises during your outdoor swimming adventures. Before sending your dog off-leash to a shoreline, examine the surrounding area. You don't want to disturb coiled snakes sunning themselves on shore rocks. Most animals taking a cool drink would rather run off than deal with such visitors. Make sure your arrival to a watering hole is loud so you don't sneak up on anything. Head for salt water if you want to avoid company.

No-Pew
De-Skunking Recipe

Immediately after your dog gets hit by a skunk, saturate him with thick plain pasta sauce or tomato juice. Usually dogs get skunked in the face, making the skin of the face and around the eyes red and inflamed. Rub the tomato into the coat, pouring sauce or juice over the worst-hit area. Let the tomato sit on the coat and rinse. Repeat. If the invading skunk has left the yard, you can put your dog outside, leaving the sauce on the coat. If not, you will have to sacrifice your clean bathroom. In parallel, or once you have initially treated the situation, make a solution of tomato juice or sauce with 3 percent hydrogen peroxide and baking soda. Apply to the affected areas, let set for a few minutes, and rinse. De-skunking with a tomato solution is an effective but messy business.

Dog Games and Play

Dogs are playful creatures that can find entertainment in even the simplest games and objects. The bow position is the universal signal a dog uses to ask you to play. Chest to the ground and behind in the air, your dog is ready for some fun. He may further encourage you to play with some friendly yaps. Some dogs like to play more with people, while others prefer the antics of their own kind. This is evident at the dog park. One dog will fixate on a game of fetch whereas another will chase his friends around, ignoring his owner. It is important to socialize with both types of companions with a variety of games and play. Games and play give your dog exercise, mental and physical challenges, and an emotional release. Classic dog games include tug-o-war, fetch, keep-away, chase, search, and wrestling. While these games are innocent enough, they are also a means of determining the pack order, such as who is stronger, faster, or smarter. When your dog is playing with other dogs, watch for signs of irritation, fatigue, or ganging up. Intervene when a game begins to spoil. Not all dogs are such good sports, and sharing toys or attention may not bode well with unfriendly Fidos.

For an out-of-yard challenge, sign your dog up for one of the many available dog sports. From obedience to free-style dancing, tracking, agility, retrieving, or hunting, there is a sport that you and your dog can have fun at together. Tracking, retrieving, and hunting sports appeal to on-the-go dogs and owners. Both owner and hound must be undaunted by weather, mud, and bugs and be willing to cover large territories of field and forest in the unpredictable great outdoors. For teams that prefer athleticism in a more controlled environment, dancing or agility sports is a good choice. Finally, obedience competition appeals to the more civilized duo. In quiet synchrony, dog and owner effortlessly carry out a pattern of command and action.

Participating in dog sports is a great way to make new friends that share your fondness for the canine persuasion. Depending on what appeals to you, you can find a sport that's entirely indoors, entirely outdoors, or both. Most sports have different skill levels to encourage amateurs to take part and begin learning. If you and your dog are real champs, try to earn titles in more than one sport, making your dog a dual or triple champion. If you are not that competitive, just share some novel activities with your friends. You can even use an activity as an excuse for throwing a party, such as a Dog Olympics party. Prepare games at your home or rent an outdoor or indoor facility that has equipment and agility courses and award medals to the top-placing pooches.

Polo Pooch

Make use of all that lovely green grass post polo season. Once the ponies have cleared the field, let your dog run about chasing the polo ball.

Wrestling Games

Clear a generous space in a carpeted room, put on some play clothes, and get down to your dog's level. Spend five minutes wrestling with your dog. Push, shove, and get a faceful of bobbing tail. Remember, to maintain your status as pack leader, it is important that you gently win this game.

Tropical Toy

For hours of outdoor fun, give your dog a hairy coconut to tear apart. You may have to get his interest by drilling a few holes, letting the coconut milk leak out. Heavy chewers love this game.

Opening Ceremony:

Parade of dogs and owners. Make sure you enlist a few bystanders to cheer the walkers on. Parade dogs by size or breed.

Obedience Competition:

Dogs are scored for best Sit, Stay, and Come.

Tracking Competition:

Dogs are scored on their ability to find ten hidden biscuits in the yard. Keep the competition fair by hiding the treats in the same ten places for each dog's run.

Fetching Competition:

Dogs are scored on their ability to retrieve a thrown ball on land or water. Better scores are given to the fastest retriever and to the dog that is able to place the ball back in the owner's hand or directly at his or her feet.

Agility Competition:

Dog and owner are judged on the team's ability to complete a course of tunnels and jumps.

Awards Ceremony:

Hand out medals for competition winners along with special prizes for best-natured dog, best beggar, and to the dog who napped the most.

If you are fortunate enough to have an in-ground pool or a friend who does, you can entertain your dog with little to no effort. Distract your dog from begging for the chops sizzling on the grill with a mechanical fish. Available at pool-supply stores, battery-operated fish will meander the swimming pool. More timid dogs will chase the fish around the pool's edge and will lean out to grab the fish on a close approach. Braver dogs will jump in over and over again and swim after the moving fish. These fish are not chew friendly, so meet your dog at the pool steps to take the fish away. Set the fish out again in the pool for another round of fun.

Spa Toys

Here is a puzzle for you: What can release tension, excite, teach, and clean teeth all at the same time? Your dog's toy! Yes, it may cost an exorbitant amount, but look what it can do! In preparation for your home spa day, survey your dog's toys. Decide which toys are ready to "go to that special place" by looking for damaged stuffed animals and rubber playthings. You don't want your dog eating squeaks or toy bits, as this could be fatal. Some plush toys can and should be washed and are salvageable with some stitching, but others should be thrown out. Because of the outrageous prices for dog toys, I often go to discount and salvage stores that sell unwanted or used children's toys. I get great new toys for one to two dollars, and the money I save allows me to buy more toys more often. Watch out for the durability and hazards that any toy, whether made specifically for dogs or children, could present, and be sure to take a toy away once damaged. Pick a variety of new (to you) toys to have on hand for spa day: something that bounces, something that can be chewed or tugged or filled with a treat, a Frisbee, something that makes a noise when crushed or "killed." Then leave a selection around the house in interesting locations to keep your dog entertained.

Toy Safety

What's better than a ball? Well, two balls of course! Avoid small balls and toys with small parts that can be torn off. These pose choking hazards or can be swallowed and become stuck in the digestive tract. Consuming jagged toy parts or bone shards can hurt your dog. Also think about the materials your dog is chewing. Do the soft plastic toys contain chemicals such as polyvinyl chloride that could leach into your pet's mouth? Some leather products are laden with chemicals from the tanning process. Maybe someday soon, we'll see a special aisle in pet stores dedicated to safety-tested products for dogs.

When selecting a toy, consider your dog's preferences, size, and habit. Does your dog like to hunt, retrieve, or chew? Do you have a large dog that could accidentally swallow a small ball? Is your dog a heavy chewer that needs a virtually indestructible toy? Is your dog afraid of noisy things? Pick toys that are size and style appropriate and that engage your pet. The dogs in the picture on page 86 have partially deflated the soccer ball, making it easier to carry and less likely to hurt their teeth. Remember that, with age and/or improper dental care, dogs can get loose teeth, making hard objects painful to bite.

Most toys are made to satisfy chewing or chasing needs but are not geared toward more intellectual stimulation. But increasingly, dog toys are being designed with more sophistication. Toys come with a variety of sounds, hardness, sizes, and materials, but the best toys require some problem solving. Dogs love toys that have puzzles and can hold their interest. There are toys that hold small treats or are stuffed with smaller toys inside. In the wild, there are lots of problems that dogs must overcome, so be creative and look around the house for interesting objects. I took a large clear plastic tub with a plastic latch and put food inside. My dogs could see where I put the food and were entertained by the biscuits rolling around as they tried to find a way to open the tub. Finally, my younger dog learned to use her nose to undo the latch. Using the same skill set, she also learned how to open the back door, so she lets herself in the house when she is ready to come in. Now, she needs to learn how to close the door.

Do It Yourself
Great homemade toys include frozen rags wrapped like a pretzel, cardboard boxes, and empty plastic soda bottles with the cap and plastic ring removed. Have more fun still and hide a liver snack with a new toy and wrap it with a piece of tissue paper. Your family can take photographs as your dog gleefully unwraps his home spa toy. This German shepard is enjoying a modified game of bobbing for apples. His friend below is playing the same game in a huge puddle.

Chapter 7: Good Nutrition

Commercial Feeds

You're on Atkins. What's your dog on? Nonfat, low-carb? Some people watch everything they put in their mouth but pay little attention to what they feed their dog. Wear your dog's shoes for a moment and imagine eating the same thing day in and day out. Is what you are serving expensive but made of substandard ingredients? A dog food made of fillers, by-products, and preservatives? Take a moment to read, from start to finish, the label of your dog food brand. Look past the advertising. If you do not have a lot of time, read the first two ingredients listed. Examples of good first ingredients are lamb, turkey, chicken, and venison. Look for solid second ingredients like brown rice, potatoes, or barley. Some high-quality feeds to consider are Artemis, California Natural, Innova, and Wellness brands. While the perfect content and proportion of commercial ingredients is as controversial as it is for humans, there are some manufacturers that are doing a good job of producing decent dog food.

Most of your pet-owner budget will go toward purchasing dog food. Large-breed owners take the biggest financial hit, purchasing vast quantities of expensive kibble. If you are attached to the convenience of commercial dog food, serve the brand that is made of the best ingredients. Do not get ripped off by paying a lot of money for poor content. Most dog foods have long lists of ingredients, which, on one hand, provide great variety. However, on the other hand, the same variety can pose problems for dogs with food allergies. If your dog has food allergies (typically to corn or wheat), watch out for complicated feeds until you can pinpoint the allergen. Also related to ingredients, do not be fooled by tricky product labels. Remember, dog food ingredients are listed on the label from greatest in content to least. Look for meat as the first ingredient. Companies use clever recipes to push the meat ingredient up the label ladder. Let's say you own Pooch Foods and have a dog food that contains 1 pound (455 g) of meat and 2 pounds (910 g) of corn, making corn the first ingredient listed. You could push meat to first place by replacing the 2 pounds (910 g) of corn with $\frac{1}{2}$ pound (225 g) each of corn, wheat, rice, and barley. If the first two or three major ingredients are meat, it is a good sign.

If you are uncomfortable with feeding your dog an entirely "people food" diet, help stretch the life of the kibble bag by adding in fresh food. Healthy extras like unsweetened yogurt, bananas, peas, and, if you are feeling adventurous, a raw chicken leg will nicely supplement commercial feed. (While cooked poultry bones are generally not considered safe to give your dog, the bone in a raw chicken leg will not splinter, so it doesn't pose a health hazard.) To reduce the risk of salmonella infection, briefly boil raw meat before serving and introduce new foods in small quantities to avoid adverse reactions. Consider introducing $\frac{1}{4}$ cup (50-75 g) portions of new fruits and vegetables, and monitor your dog's reaction. Dogs can eat uncooked bones, but again, limit the initial size. His eyes will be bigger than his stomach.

Does Your Dog Have an Allergy?

Is your dog constantly scratching his ears or coat, or does he have sores and bumps on his coat? Unfortunately, determining the source of an allergy can be very difficult. Dogs can have seasonal allergies, food allergies, or reactions to an indoor allergen or chemical. Work with your veterinarian to deduce the problem through the process of elimination. Think about when the reaction started. In addition to medical intervention, take steps at home to improve your dog's health by switching to allergen-free bedding and hypoallergenic detergents and by running an air filter. If you suspect a food allergy, switch to a dog food for allergy-prone pets.

A Dog Food Myth

Some people think they should never vary their dog's kibble. They're wrong. If you can't decide on which kibble to serve, don't limit your dog to just one. Vary the kibble by the type of first meat ingredient. Give chicken kibble for breakfast and duck kibble for dinner.

Whole Foods Menu

Feeding dogs a raw diet of uncooked, unprocessed foods is the newest, old idea. The current dogma that "people food" is bad for dogs is a fallacy. Since when did meat, fruit, vegetables, and grains become just for people to consume? When were dogs relegated to eating pellets that are unrecognizable, rendered forms of original fresh food? Before dogs became kept modern pets, they subsisted on raw meat and whatever else they came across that was edible. Your grandmother probably did not haul home huge bags of kibble; canned and bagged commercial dog food is a modern invention that is promoted by expensive marketing. Commercial dog food is big business.

Switch, even in part, to a raw diet, providing foods that are closest to their original, unaltered forms and are full of healthy vitamins, minerals, and other nutrients and enzymes. Feed your dog raw animal meat and organs, meaty bones, fish, fruit, vegetables, beans, certain live-culture or Lactaid-treated dairy products (adult dogs, like people, can be lactose intolerant), a little honey, and grains. You will find that certain meat selections are very inexpensive. Fruits and vegetables, such as bananas, carrots, and cabbage are also very affordable. You will spend equal to or less money serving a raw diet, and you will be providing a superior meal.

There is often misinformation about giving dogs bones. If the meat is uncooked, your dog can eat the bone, but if the meat is cooked, remove the bone. Your dog will not choke from eating raw animal bones. Dogs like eating rubbery, crunchy raw bones. It is healthy for them and keeps their teeth clean. When you give your dog a raw meaty bone, nothing goes to waste.

To sterilize the surface of raw meat, I use a designated set of stainless steel tongs and submerge the meat in boiling water for about thirty seconds. I then let the meat cool briefly before serving. To further prevent the spread of food-borne illness, I treat my dog's raw meat with the same care I treat the cutting board I use to prepare my own uncooked meats. I wash my dog's bowls and serving tongs in the dishwasher and put their meals outside or in a separate room. This is because, occasionally, they like to drag their meal out of the bowl and hold it between their paws while they eat on the floor. Choose a dining floor that is bleach-cleaning friendly, like tile.

Mother Nature's Meal

My dogs are 65 and 75 pounds (29.5 and 34 kg). Here is an example of a meal they like to eat: Four raw plump chicken legs, six Brussels sprouts, ½ sweet potato each. You will need to experiment to determine your dog's appropriate portion size and favorite foods. I recommend introducing a small amount of a new food as a snack. If your dog has been eating the same commercial feed for years, you will have to wean him off of it unless he responds well to a cold-turkey change. Unlike puppies, adult dogs have more difficulty accepting new foods.

Spa Food Planning

Purchase seven durable plastic meal containers with or without divided sections and seven small containers for storing a raw meat portion that will be boiled quickly prior to serving. Using indelible ink, label the container lids with the seven days of the week. Once you have done your weekly grocery shopping, fill the dog food containers with a variety of foods. Banana sections, broccoli, corn, yogurt, yams, raw meat and organ meat, and so forth. If you are short on time, add canned or frozen vegetables to the fresh food mix. By planning a week's worth of food, you can consider the variety you are offering and correct portion size. You will keep preparation and cooking mess to a minimum and will save time during the week. When your dog is ready to eat, add the boiled meat to the larger prefilled container and serve. Some dogs get a reaction to eating from plastic dishes, so you can also opt to put the meal contents in a stainless steel dish. Place the used containers in the dishwasher for cleaning.

Gourmet Meals

Admit it, your dog begs at the table because, every now and then, he gets lucky, and you share your table food with him. Or maybe you feed your dog strictly kibble, but he has compensated by expertly snapping up fallen bits or surfing the countertops to steal available munchies. Instead of cheating, scolding, or feeling guilty, every blue moon, declare defeat and cook enough for two. For those extra-, extra-special occasions, consider the following gourmet breakfast, lunch, and dinner menus for your spa dog. Double the portions if your dog will be sharing with you.

Fit Frappe
Combine half a bag of mixed frozen berries (blueberries, raspberries, and blackberries) with enough reduced-sugar juice or plain yogurt to blend. Serve 1 cup (230 g) of this healthy, creamy smoothie for a lip-licking treat.

Spa Menu
—Bon appétit—

Breakfast

Spa breakfast:
$\frac{1}{4}$ cup (65 g) mixed fresh berries and melon cubes with two organic, scrambled eggs

Wellness breakfast:
1 cup (230 g) cooled cooked oatmeal topped with walnuts and baked apple slices

Hearty breakfast:
$\frac{1}{3}$ cup (85 g) cooled grits sprinkled with Cheddar cheese and low-salt ham; one pancake topped with banana

Lunch

Spa lunch:
One ripe avocado, pit removed; 1 cup (230 g) mixed steamed vegetables such as broccoli and cauliflower; one deboned broiled chicken breast

Wellness lunch:
Deboned grilled fish fillet with $\frac{1}{3}$ cup (85 g) long-grain rice and mango slices

Hearty lunch:
Grilled apple sections and turkey cutlet with a dollop of chunky cranberry sauce with toasted wholegrain bread slice

Dinner

Spa dinner:
$\frac{1}{3}$ cup (85 g) vegetable couscous, steamed salmon fillet

Wellness dinner:
1 cup (230 g) whole wheat pasta with lean turkey Bolognese sauce and a mixed salad

Hearty dinner:
1 cup (230 g) collard greens, juicy cooked pork chop (bone removed), dirty mashed potatoes mixed with unsweetened yogurt

Dessert

Spa dessert:
Frozen Lactaid milk slush (The Lactaid will prevent lactose-intolerance symptoms in a dog sensitive to dairy products.)

Wellness dessert:
Tapioca mixed in kefir

Hearty dessert:
Low-sugar carrot-zucchini-banana bread

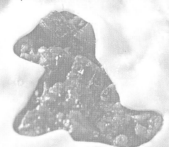

Water

If you remember your school science lessons, we are all basically bags of salty water. As bags of mostly salty water, you and your dog have a lot in common (i.e., you both need to stay well hydrated to perform normal tissue and cellular functions). No water, big problem. Since water is essential for life, give your dog access to fresh water at all times. Not sometimes, not once a day, even if it runs out or ends up on the floor; all the time. Change the water a few times each day (flushing the toilet is not what I mean by changing the water). Fill big bowls both upstairs and downstairs (and outside if you leave your dog in the yard). Should you fail to notice that a bowl is empty, the second bowl will serve as a backup water supply. It is very common for dogs to spill the water in their bowls or to drink an entire bowl after exercising. Clean the water bowls regularly. Even stainless steel bowls get dirty. Always keep a jug of water with you in the car. Offer your dog water at the start of your walk and especially at the end, before you drive home. This will deter your dog from drinking outdoor water that could contain parasites. Your dog will drink to stay healthy but must be able to get to clean water throughout the day.

Teach your dog to tell you when the water bowl is empty. Each time you fill the bowl, gently touch a bell to your dog's nose. Praise your dog. Make sure you use the bell softly against the nose so as not to startle your dog. Hang the bell low to the ground near the bowl and fill the bowl with water. Your dog will learn that by ringing the bell, he can make sure the bowl gets filled. You can buy big holiday bells in gold or silver tone, in large sizes or grape clusters that are easy for a dog to push or paw at. I don't recommend using this trick for filling the kibble bowl, unless you want to hear bells ringing all day long.

Herbs and Supplements

Ever catch your dog grazing in the yard, eating dirt or licking metal or rocks? Well, your pooch may be doing his own version of selecting beneficial herbs or supplementing his deficient diet. The use of herbs and supplements with dogs is very controversial. Many veterinarians find the use of vitamins, herbs, and other supplements not only ineffective, but also potentially toxic and dangerous. Even favorites like brewer's yeast and chamomile have reportedly caused allergic reactions in people and pets. That said, and since isolated incidents of toxicity can overwhelm a history of safe and effective use, I recommend you research any food additive you are considering so you are knowledgeable about the benefits and reported side effects. Consult the expertise of specialists and organizations versed in natural pet care. Review the Food and Drug Administration's Generally Regarded as Safe list for foods, herbs, and oils that are believed by the government to be safe for use. Since many store-bought supplements distill out and concentrate certain elements of a plant, it is better to provide the supplementation in its original, edible form. For example, serve your dog a variety of fresh greens and vegetables to allow him to benefit from different plants' anticancer properties. Dogs love eating fresh Brussels sprouts and cabbage greens. A polite word of caution: about two hours later, your house will smell like an Irish dinner, so don't serve these vegetables before house-guests arrive. Begin your exploration into pet wellness with treatments you are most comfortable with. Try soothing an itchy coat with an oatmeal bath and olive oil rinse. Add a tablespoon of salmon oil and chopped garlic to your dog's kibble. Dab aloe vera on a scrape or insect bite. Since your dog cannot speak, remain vigilant for ailments that require your assistance in the form of natural or pharmaceutical remedies. Use natural foods and herbs and a solid diet as your pet's first line of defense against illness and to promote superior health.

Various Herbs Used by Holistic Veterinarians

Herb	What It's Used For
Aloe	*Minor burns, skin irritations, stomach disorders*
Borage	*Fever, inflammation, respiratory infections, stress*
Bupleurum	*Fever, irritability*
Chamomile	*Anxiety, flatulence, indigestion, inflammation, healing of wounds*
Comfrey	*Bruises, burns, ulcers, healing wounds (for external use only)*
Echinacea	*Viral and bacterial illness, eczema, skin problems*
Fennel	*Colic, flatulence, indigestion, coughs*
Garlic	*Common cold, cough, adenoid problems, respiratory infections, bacterial infections*
Ginger	*Motion sickness, dizziness, digestion*
Goldenseal	*Digestion, inflammation, infection*
Hawthorn	*Insomnia, heart trouble, nervousness*
Lavender	*Nervous exhaustion, insomnia, rheumatic pain*
Marigold	*Bruises, burns, healing wounds, skin inflammation, conjunctivitis, some fungal infections, adenoid problems*
Milk Thistle	*Liver disorders, psoriasis*
Mullen	*Diarrhea, hemorrhoids, bronchitis, coughs*
Nettle	*Constipation, allergies*
Peppermint	*Indigestion, nausea*
Red Raspberry	*Diarrhea, nausea, vomiting*
Rosemary	*Headache, muscular pain, neuralgia, general debility, digestive problems*
Tangerine Peel	*Peel Digestion*
White Willow	*Fever and inflammation*
Yarrow	*Wounds, high blood pressure*

Nature's Remedy

Does your pup get green around the gills? Car sickness is a common dog ailment. Before you travel, feed your dog some bland salted crackers sprinkled with brewer's yeast. Put a bundle of fresh peppermint in front of the car air vents and circulate cool air while traveling. These home remedies will help ease your dog's motion sickness naturally.

Vegetables are a welcome addition to your pet's diet. Dogs will rouge their muzzles eating cold borscht soup, a mealtime favorite that combines a variety of healthful vegetables chock full of antioxidants and vitamins. If you don't have time to make traditional borscht, mash cooked beets, whole red potatoes, cabbage, apple, parsley, carrots, and celery in chicken broth. Add a dab of sour cream for an authentic touch. Set the bowl down and watch the colorful stew disappear.

A natural approach to flea control is a welcome remedy for any dog owner. Fill a section of cheese cloth or coffee filter with pennyroyal, peppermint, and lavender. Steep the mixture in 1 quart (0.95 L) hot water. Allow the solution to cool. Wet a cotton ball with the mixture and patch test it on a small area of skin on your dog's inner thigh. Check the tested area the next day for any reaction or redness. If your dog passes the patch test, sponge the bug repellent over your dog's coat, let it air-dry, and head off to the park.

Treats and Chews

You thought it would never happen, but it did. Yes, you can now buy energy bars for your dog. No time for a breakfast bowl of kibble? Try a food bar for your busy, on-the-go pooch. You have come to accept the existence of doggy breath mints but this takes everything to a new low or high, depending on how you view these innovations. Regardless of your level of interest, there are a variety of treats available for your dog. Read the ingredient list and select biscuits and bites made of high-quality ingredients. There seems to be an inverse relationship between treats that look the most like doggy versions of human food and the quality of the treat. Beware of supermarket shelves that are chock full of these gimmicky, low-quality snacks. Remember to limit calories from biscuit snacks to maintain a lean dog. Try giving tiny bits of treats, carrots, or frozen vegetables to limit calories. Freeze-dried liver snacks are a great training treat and can be purchased additive- and preservative-free.

Obesity by Biscuit
Watch out for those extra calories from treats. Make sure your biscuits are of good food quality, and remember to keep the calories down if your dog is plump.

Natural Chew
Uncooked animal bones do not splinter and are edible for dogs. Visit the butcher and select a meaty uncooked bone full of yummy marrow. Boil for thirty seconds in water and serve. To avoid your dog dragging or, worse yet, trying to hide his bone around the house, give it as an outdoor snack.

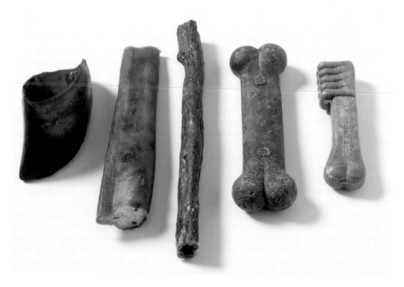

Chews can be made from natural ingredients (such as hardened foods, fibers, or animal parts) or man—made substances such as plastic, rubber, and nylon. Natural products include rawhide in all shapes, colors, and sizes; bones; ears; snouts; hooves; muscles; and private parts, to name a few. Look for animal parts that are sterilized, will not splinter easily, and are unbleached. Oh, you didn't know that chews can be bleached? Make sure the chew passes the "What is it?" test. If you can't tell what the chew is made of, do not buy it. Keep in mind that just because there are the words "chicken," "beef," or "cheese" on the label, does not mean the chew is not synthetic. While you should never let your dog eat nonfood items, it is acceptable for dogs to chew on indestructible dog-safe materials like ropes and certain superhard plastics that cannot be broken down and swallowed. You cannot protect your dog from every health hazard, but exercise common sense. Chewing is a very important part of a dog's way of life, just like talking is for people. Dogs relieve tension by chewing, so if you do not provide chews, your dog may nibble shoes and furniture.

Quick Homemade Biscotti

Ingredients

1 egg
1 cup (140g) store-bought corn muffin mix
3 cups (675 ml) water
1 cup (120g) whole wheat flour
1 lb. (455g) raw pureed beef liver

Directions

1. Place all ingredients in a large bowl. Mix thoroughly to combine.

2. Spread mixture in a shallow baking sheet and bake in a 350°F (175°C) oven until firm (about 10-15 minutes).

3. Remove tray from the oven and cut the cake into rectangles. Place the biscotti on a baking sheet and allow treats to bake a second time by turning the oven off and leaving the biscuits to harden in the cooling oven for a few hours.

Gingerbones

Ingredients

4 cups (920 g) all-purpose flour
2 cups (460 g) whole wheat flour
1 cup (230 g) molasses
1 cup (240 ml) water
$\frac{1}{2}$ cup (120 ml) vegetable oil
4 tablespoon (60 ml) ground ginger
2 teaspoons (10 ml) ground cinnamon
1 teaspoon (5 ml) ground cloves

Directions

1. Place all ingredients in a large bowl. Mix thoroughly to combine.

2. Roll out dough on floured surface to about $\frac{1}{4}$-inch (6 mm) thick. Using a cookie cutter, cut into bone shapes. Combine dough scraps and continue to roll out and cut into shapes until all dough has been used.

3. Place cookies on ungreased foil-lined baking sheets, and bake in a preheated 325° (170°C) oven for 30 to 35 minutes. Makes 5 to 6 dozen cookies.

Dogs love the taste and aroma of their very own gingery cookie.

How Much Should Fido Weigh?

Consult breed standards, which have acceptable weight ranges for both males and slightly smaller females. Another way is to feel how much fat is deposited over the rib cage. You should be able to feel individual ribs, and the body should taper slightly at the waist.

Home Spa Dog Promises

➤ I will assume responsibility for the well-being of my dog.
➤ I will endeavor to provide clean water and wholesome food to my dog.
➤ I will provide my dog with daily aerobic exercise.
➤ I will engage my dog with the community, participating in play groups, sports, or social activities.
➤ I will develop my dog's intellectual capabilities.
➤ I will open up my heart to my dog.

Weight-Control Regimens

Is Fido F-A-T? Did your cutie evolve from svelte puppy to butterball? You hadn't really noticed the extra weight, except that your buddy has slowed down on walks. He really likes those cookie-sized doggy treats. They're loaded with fat and sugar, but they're affordable. Your veterinarian mentioned that Fido is "too heavy for his frame," so you decreased his kibble ration and that has turned him into a nonstop begging professional. You cannot stand his whining and give in to his demands. You feed his boredom, and your guilt, with biscuits.

Pet obesity in this country is rampant, and we have only ourselves to blame. Did you know that animals fed fewer calories live considerably longer than their overfed counterparts? With some large breeds having a life expectancy of only ten years, wouldn't you want to give your dog the healthiest, longest life possible? The good news is that it is very easy to take excess weight off a dog because you can control his portion size, quality of food, and activity level. You and your dog can successfully make a health improvement and reduce illness and disease through good nutrition.

Steps to Taking the Weight Off

- Measure how many cups of kibble you are giving your dog. Check that the amount matches the recommended portion size. If you have been giving your dog too large a portion, gradually reduce the amount to the recommended allowance.
- Call a family meeting and talk about how many treats are being fed collectively. Agree to put a few treats each day in a jar and ask family members to pull from the daily ration. Break the treats into tiny pieces to stretch the snacks. This will prevent excess snack calories.
- Switch from giving large cookie-style treats to tiny liver bits and fresh, crunchy carrots. Dogs love earning even a small bit of food.
- To keep the nutrient intake adequate, consider switching to a low-calorie kibble.
- Most importantly, increase playtime or get your pup involved in a sport.

Evaluating Your Dog's Weight

How skinny is "pretty skinny"? How heavy is "not as thin as he should be"? These guidelines provide a uniform way to describe a pet's weight, from "emaciated" to "grossly obese".

How Does Your Dog Measure Up?

Underweight Her ribs are visible with minimal fat cover. Bony prominences (hips, shoulders) are easily felt with minimal overlying fat. There is marked abdominal tuck when she is viewed from the side and a marked hourglass shape when viewed from above.

Ideal Her ribs are easily palpable with a slight fat cover. Bony prominences can be felt through a small amount of overlying fat. There is an abdominal tuck when she is viewed from the side and well-proportioned waist when viewed from above.

Overweight Her ribs are difficult to feel because the fat cover is thicker but the bony structure can still be felt. Bony prominences are covered by a moderate layer of fat. There is little or no abdominal tuck or waist when she is viewed from the side and her back is slightly broadened when viewed from above. A slight pot belly, or rounding of the abdomen, is present.

Obese Her ribs are difficult to feel because of the thick covering of fat. Bony prominences are also covered by a moderate to thick layer of fat. There is a pendulous bulge in her tummy and no waist when she is viewed from the side. Her back is markedly broadened when viewed from above. Fat deposits can also found on her face and limbs.

Weight Creep

It happens to you, and it happens to your dog. A pound or two added with each passing year culminates in middle-age plumpness and old-age obesity. Dogs mellow with age, become more sedentary and arthritic, all of which contribute to weight gain. Win the battle of the bulge by monitoring your dog's weight at each veterinary visit, adjusting food calories, and finding safe and comfortable activities your older dog will enjoy. For older dogs, you may want to massage and stretch your pet before exercising and provide shorter, more frequent bouts of activity. Consider walking on grass instead of hard pavement surfaces.

Make sure to assert your status as alpha dog at mealtime. Your dog is a pack animal and views your family as his pack. He will feel comforted knowing you are in charge and will be frustrated by inconsistent messages that tell him he is top dog. To maintain your status as household leader, feed your dog after you have finished eating. When you are done with your meal, give your dog a small table scrap. If you do not allow your dog to eat "human food," fill the kibble bowl only when dinner is over. Your dog will expect and respect this.

It is normal canine behavior for a dog to bury extra goodies to keep for a later snack. Maybe your dog not only hides treats in the backyard but has gotten a little creative in the house. I have found biscuits hidden under pillows, in blankets, behind sofa cushions, and in my work bag. Finding the perfect hiding spot will keep you entertained and keep your dog busy and focused.

How Much Should You Feed Your Dog?

The answer really depends on your dog's current weight for his frame, his food intake, and his activity level.

1. Is your dog currently under- or overweight?
2. How much food is your dog currently eating? Is the serving size less or more than recommended?
3. How active is your dog? If your dog is too skinny, offer him additional servings of healthy food during the day. If your dog is overweight, gently increase his playtime, and if in excess, reduce calories beginning with a common culprit, biscuits.

Chapter 8: Spa Living

Establishing a Routine

To live the home spa life with your dog year-round, select the essential elements or habits for you and your pet, and determine their necessary frequency. This will allow you to establish a routine. Use the changing seasons to add variety to your dog's life while maintaining a foundation of good habits such as feeding high-quality meals, daily exercise, ear cleaning, and so forth. Your good habits will not only optimize your relationship with your dog, but also will reduce medical bills and psychological problems. In the "Good Habits" section are important home spa activities with some recommended rates of recurrence. Remember that if you fall off the wagon and become deficient in any one habit, establish some new resolutions and reward yourself for each month's accomplishments. Set reminders in your monthly calendar to help remember widely spaced activities such as monthly or quarterly events. Remember, something is better than nothing. Don't throw in the towel if you find you can't keep up. Continue to adapt your spa schedule until you find one that works with your lifestyle. Keep a dog journal. Purchase a blank writing journal, keepsake box, or scrapbook and record your best friend's development. Pat your puppy's paw on an ink pad and press on a book page. Record basic size measurements at different ages, such as weight, length, and height. Paste in favorite pictures. In the early years, write once a month about your dog's progress in learning vocabulary words. Record information about both good and bad habits. Later in life, write an entry once a quarter. List favorite biscuit recipes or foods your dog loves. Record when you first notice tooth or hip problems, hearing loss, or major illnesses. If you get another dog, especially of the same breed, you will be able to use the previous information as a benchmark and improve your caretaking.

memories of
homes you've
lived, laughed
and loved in

2005
JENN·MASON

Good Habits

A visit to a pet store can be very, very expensive. One 30-pound bag of commercial food and a few toys and you have spent eighty dollars. From the astronomical cost of pet food and toys to all the impulse extras, the bill can be pricey. To prevent over-rover-spending, set a monthly and yearly budget allowing for the costs of maintaining good habits. You will need to set aside money for food, new toys, entry fees for dog sports, new collars and leashes, linens, vaccinations, bowls, grooming, toothpaste and brush. Make a comprehensive list to accurately forecast the expenses. Write out your doggy wish list and decide where you can get the best value. For example, toothbrushes can run about one dollar in a value-pack or on sale; this is much less expensive than buying a toothbrush at a pet store. Grooming your dog yourself will save you about fifty dollars. If you find a great bargain leash, buy a few to use when the old one wears out. Save your money for a rainy day. You may need the extra money for an unexpected large expense such as an uninsured pet surgery.

Lunchtime Workout
If you work, the most loving thing you can do for your dog is pay for two hours of midday playtime, walking, and companionship. You will probably find that, if you look for an unorthodox dog walker, you can get more than the typical thirty-minute, fifteen-dollar daily walk. Put an advertisement in your local paper or ask a stay-at-home parent or retired person to play with your best friend for a few hours. You are likely to get more playtime and personal service than you would through a traditional dog walker who rotates many dogs during the day. You may be able to find someone local looking for extra income who would welcome the opportunity. Planning a midday visit, while you are at work, is a perfect way to break up your dog's day. You will return home to a well-exercised, happy, calm dog.

Daily

- Two hours of physical activity (vary based on physical ability, age, and breed)
- High-quality meals
- Toothbrushing
- Fresh water
- Affection
- Comfortable living space
- Supportive bed with clean linens
- Toys inspected for integrity
- One-on-one time with family

Weekly

- Training
- Special outdoor excursion
- Coat brushing
- Ear cleaning
- Pick up eliminations in the yard

Monthly

- Restock food, toys, and other worn supplies
- Nail trim

Quarterly

- Participate in an organized dog sport
- Bathe dog
- Spread lime pellets in backyard to neutralize dog urine odors

Semiannually

- Visit to the Veterinarian

Annually

- Birthday celebration

Training in Minutes a Day

Keep formal training sessions to five minutes. Remember, people and dogs learn better from spaced versus massed learning. That means that short, spaced training is better than long sessions where brains can get saturated with new information. Practice a few minutes once a week, and you would be surprised how much you can teach. Use the time to teach new commands or to freshen up old commands. Remember that all training should be reinforced daily by following good habits. If your dog makes a mistake 100 times, correct him 101 times. Remember that you are in charge.

Dog Sports

Participating in an organized dog sport may be a little different than you imagined. At events, be prepared to wait a lot, and do not expect your dog to play with other dogs. To prepare, take your dog for exercise before you leave the house. Usually, you will have to drive some distance, so activity ahead of time is a must. Bring snacks, water, and weather-appropriate gear such as hats, long sleeves, gloves, and bug repellent. Most importantly, bring a comfortable crate where your dog can wait for his or her turn. Most judged dog sports have very entry-level competitions that you and your dog can participate in. Enlist the help of veterans who can explain what you are supposed to do. Do not worry about failing, but prepare ahead of time. When you go to an event, the most important rule for success is that you have off-leash control of your dog. Your dog should obey, stay, and come, and be well socialized to other dogs. It may be difficult to make friends at your first dog event. Participants will do a lot of dog talk and may use vocabulary words you are not familiar with. Ask questions, keep attending and learning, and you will end up with lifelong friends. Remember that a dog sport lies somewhere in the realm between off-leash playtime and a formal obedience class. Start your dog in a sport early in life, while he or she is most adaptable and able to learn new things quickly.

Hop!

The number one complaint I hear from dog owners is that their dog jumps up on visitors. While this is a common complaint, you should still endeavor to teach the useful "Hop" command, which means to jump on. Practice "On" or "Hop" and "Off" with objects in the home (like the couch and bed) and outdoors (like picnic tables). This command will help large and giant breed owners get their dog on the examination table at the veterinary clinic. Usually, in each examination room, there is a chair and raised metal examination table. If your dog understands "Hop," you will be able to at least (1) get your dog to sit on the chair and place his front legs on the table while you lift the rear end onto the table, or (2) from the floor, you will be able to get your dog to put his front legs on the table while you lift the back end up. It is much easier when your dog is working with you to get onto the table than if you have to lift your dog up yourself entirely. Most dogs will not be comfortable placing their feet on the metal table, so you will have to steady your pet.

Throw Your Dog a Birthday Party

You have two options when planning your invitation list. You can invite your friends and all their dogs, or you can limit the invitation to your friends and only one to three tried-and-true doggy friends. Having a large dog party will be tricky and not very relaxing. The dogs will be stressed and could compete for territory and food. If your dog is not used to a lot of excitement, throw a party with just one favored playmate, allowing your dog to be the center of attention. In addition to the usual fare needed for a human party, add the following items for your dog's birthday party: children's party hats, balloons, a doggy birthday cake with mashed potato frosting, dog-themed decorations and food, a dog game like bobbing for tennis balls or a biscuit hunt in the yard. Pile your guests' gifts together, and let your dog tear open his presents. Remember to take pictures. Have covered crates available for guests to let their dogs rest, and remember to put safety first, keeping exits secure and designating someone as the undistracted doggy nanny. Count how many of your guests have dogs, cats, or other pets themselves; prepare bags of take-home favors filled with dog toys, bones, or other appropriate pet gifts.

Recipe for a Doggy Birthday Cake

Preheat oven to 350°F (180°C). Mix 1 pound (455 g) ground beef, 1 beaten egg, $\frac{1}{4}$ cup (60 g) Cream of Wheat, $\frac{1}{4}$ cup (60 g) mashed carrots, and 2 tablespoons (30 ml) water. Shape the mixture into a loaf in a greased cake mold for baking. Bake until cooked through, about 40 minutes. Unmold the loaf onto a serving dish and allow to cool. "Frost" with mashed potatoes.

A Dog's Calendar for the Seasons

January

Schedule a visit to the veterinarian. Start off New Year's Day with some Doggy Yoga. Find a dog-friendly superstore and walk around for some warm indoor exercise.

April

Shop for and pack a first-aid kit for car and home. Play bobbing for tennis balls in a large puddle or in a tub of water. Head into the city for an on-leash weekend walk around people and stores.

February

Take a break from the winter doldrums. Enroll your dog in an indoor agility class. Give your dog a massage for Valentine's Day.

May

April was wet and rainy; invest in a new collar and lead. Volunteer at an animal charity or host a rescue dog. Shop at a large garden center with your best friend—so many trees, so little time.

March

Spring cleaning. Throw out old bedding and weathered toys. Go with your dog to a big pet-supply store and restock the toy bin. Find an empty public swing set and hit the slides with your dog. Practice obedience training with some biscuit hopscotch. Fido must wait patiently for the biscuit while you hop the course.

June

Purchase some floating dummies, and practice water retrieving. Shoot flower-laden pictures of your dog. Save the best picture for your winter holiday cards. Go to an outdoor restaurant. Take your dog on a postdinner promenade.

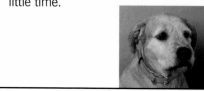

July

Schedule a visit to the veterinarian. Hire a professional trainer for an obedience refresher. Take your dog for a joy ride.

October

Build a leaf pile for your dog to play in. Visit the pumpkin patch. Bake some homemade pumpkin dog biscuits. Take your dog trick-or-treating with the kids.

August

It's the dog days of summer. Head out for some cool lake swimming. Have a doggy sleepover and invite a favored playmate. Find a dog-friendly hotel and go on vacation.

November

Order a cold-weather coat. Gobble, gobble. Go on a post-Thanksgiving hike looking for wild Turkeys that got away. Try painting your dog's portrait.

September

Beaches start opening to dogs. Walk on the shore and dig in the sand. Last chance for an outdoor bath. Go to a dog show to learn about your dog's specific breed and pick up tips from breeders and vendors.

December

Gift wrap some special presents, and let your dog open his own gifts. Build a snowman with your dog. Plan your pet-related New Year's resolutions.

Spa Gifts

Store-bought gifts are always appreciated, but you can make some luxurious dog-friendly spa products in bulk to share with friends. Here are some great seasonal gift basket ideas that your friends will rave about and their dogs will love too.

Summertime-Skunk Rescue Shampoo

At dusk in the summer, the neighborhood skunks emerge from their dens, roaming yards for grubs and food-laden trash bags. Unfortunately, curious dogs often become the victims of visiting skunks. Take advantage of the bounty of ripened tomatoes at the end of the summer to make a de-skunk shampoo for your friends with dogs.

Can tomatoes fresh from your garden or a farmer's market. Start by boiling the sliced tomatoes until you have a uniform sauce. You can spoon out the tomato skins or strain out both skin and seeds with a sieve. Pour your saucy creation into large, sterilized glass jars and seal. You can add some heirloom tomato varieties and give your de-skunking shampoo a fancy label featuring a name like Purple Tomato Passion Dog Shampoo. Put the jar in a decorative wooden box with a small jar of 3 percent hydrogen peroxide and a matching jar of gentle shampoo. Make sure all contents are properly labeled. To the largest tomato jar attach a tag with instructions explaining emergency de-skunking methods. Your friends will store your gift until they have a skunk emergency and call you afterward with sincere thanks.

Fall Harvest Candy Apple Toy

Core fresh, hard apples, removing the poisonous seeds. Melt carob chips over low heat in a double boiler, dipping the apple to coat all or part of the outer surface. If you'd like, you can use a spoon to drizzle the carob over the apple in a decorative pattern. You can also use a small piece from another apple to plug the bottom hole before dipping the apple in the carob. Sprinkle the cooling surface with dry oats. Fill the empty core with low-sugar, organic peanut butter or some other goody. Wrap the candied apple toys in cellophane and finish with a beautiful ribbon. Keep refrigerated so they will stay fresh. This is a snack that is fun for dogs to explore, and it keeps their mouths and paws busy.

Winter Cold Weather Cure

Wind, water, freezing temperatures, and dry indoor heat take their toll on a dog's skin, paws, and coat. Prepare a relief basket for a friend in need with a new towel, a bottle of apricot oil or paw balm for sore feet, and a jar of dry milk and oatmeal for a moisturizing soap-free bath. For a personalized touch, have the towel monogrammed with the dog's name or initials. Make a batch of reduced-sugar gingerbread man cookies and punch a small hole in one one of the gingerbread man's hands while warm. Let harden and attach to the package with a string for a holiday biscuit treat.

Spring No-Bug Soak

After a long winter indoors, we rush off to enjoy the outdoors and find that fleas and ticks have already arrived. For an adorable springtime gift, prepare a small, decorative plastic bucket or glass container with a high-quality sea sponge and bundles of antipest sachets. To make the sachets, cut clean coffee filters or mesh cloth into large squares. Place $\frac{1}{2}$ cup (110 g) of dried herbs and flowers known for their bug-repellent qualities in the center of the cloth squares. Dried lavender, rosemary, and cloves are all good choices. Close the sachets with a tie made of cooking twine and attach a paper label. Place the sea sponge and at least three bundles in the bucket with instructions to fill the bucket with warm water and soak a sachet in it. Sponge the liquid over the dog's coat and allow to air-dry. Head off to the park!

Heirlooms

Preserve keepsakes from the home spa days with your dog. They will become beautiful family heirlooms. Depending on your skill set, available time, and financial resources, you can create an heirloom that fits your needs and adds unique beauty to your family life. Make a scented bone-shaped pillow for your dog to rest his sleepy head on. Borrow it from him when you need some pampering. Sew him a perfectly sized dog coat or a bed cover that complements the decor. If you're more ambitious, build him a designer doghouse. For an easy creation, frame a favorite portrait of your dog. Any special heirloom you create, no matter how big or small, will add lasting richness to your life with your dog. Choose a project that's fun and rewarding to you.

Window Box

To commemorate your puppy's first year, professionally frame his tiny puppy collar, paw print, and a picture of him together for display. I like to display a collection of leather leads from each of my dogs. Another great treasure for keeping is your dog's first toy. One of my dogs has a stuffed animal I named the "provincial chicken." As a pup, the chicken and he were inseparable. Many toys have come and gone, but I saved his beloved chicken along with his sister's gray elephant. They are too big for framing but can be stored in a keepsake chest. For additional memories, make a video when you first pick up your puppy; include the car ride home, the first night at home, and other memorable moments from these early times together. Continue to take videos of your dog on his spa retreats.

Bone Pillow

Sew a fragrant dog-bone pillow for years of use in your home spa for your dog. Cut a large dog-bone pattern out of two pieces of silk. You can print a dog bone pattern from the Internet onto a large piece of paper for tracing. Sew the edges together inside out, and turn right-side out when almost sewn shut. Fill the fabric bone with buckwheat hulls and dried lavender buds. Finish sewing the pillow opening closed. To extend the life of the pillow, construct a slightly larger outer pillow with a zipper for easy cleaning. Omit the zipper, and the pillow can be warmed gently in the microwave. If you are really crafty, embroider your dog's name on the outer pillow.

Couture Coat

Create a perfectly sized retreat coat that rivals any store-bought jacket. Measure your dog from the front of his shoulder to the base of his tail. Then measure the length from the top of the knee over the back to the other knee. The two measurements will give you the dimensions of a rectangle, since dogs are longer in body length than tall from top line to knee. Choose a lining and an exterior coat fabric. Choose colors that complement the color of your dog's fur. The lining should be made from a warm and cozy material. Mark a rectangle of the proper size on each fabric. Place them over your dog to check for size before actually cutting the rectangle. (Sometimes an inch difference in length can change how the coat falls over the dog.) Simply sew the two pieces of selected material together to form the coat. Place the coat over your dog's back and measure the length required for a front chest panel. The chest panel, also a rectangle, will connect the coat in front leaving room for a neck opening. The lower edge of the chest panel should align with the bottom of the main coat. The last element is to attach a 1-inch (2.5-cm) thick strap under the chest to hold the body of the jacket in place during movement. You

can make the strap out of the same coat materials for a perfect match. I recommend experimenting with strap position and length by attaching it with safety pins to optimize fit before the final sewing. Straps that are too loose will be ineffective, and straps that are too far forward or back will cause the coat to slide to one side. Once you have tested a safety-pinned strap, affix it permanently by button, latch, or Velcro.

Pet Portrait

Nothing beams "I love my dog" more than a pet portrait on a mantel or side table. There are many ways you can create a pet portrait, even if you don't consider yourself artistically inclined. Make a photograph of your dog into a slide and project the image onto a canvas to trace. Fill in with color. You can also, using computer graphics, alter a scanned pet picture into a cartoon or black-and-white image. Simply print onto the paper size of your choice and paint. Finally, you can send a favorite picture to a commercial company to have it transformed into a paint-by-numbers canvas. Pretty neat, and you don't have to let on to your amazed friends that you had some help. Lastly, if you have the funds, hire a professional artist or photographer to create a portrait of your pet. Pick an artist who specializes in animal portraiture and has an artistic style you prefer.

Spa Trends on the Horizon

Fresh dog food at the grocer's, luxury dog spas, and nine-to-five dog schools are on their way to a city near you, making it even easier to pamper your dog in and out of your home. Based on current trends, here are a few of the improvements you can expect or hope to see in the next few years.

Designer Toys

Tired of unsightly toys strewn across the living room? Famous designers will make signature playthings with panache. Toys will still jingle and roll, but the materials, shapes, and colors will be more sophisticated and mature. Don't tell me you were attached to neon pink porcupines and rubber hamburgers! Pet stores will dedicate an aisle to organic foods and treats and dog-friendly pet toys. Free from dangerous materials, these toys will meet specified veterinary safety standards.

Identification Chips

Lose your dog? Not for long. Lost dogs will become a rarity in the near future. Traditional tags and tattooing will become outdated, low-tech accessories, replaced by identification chips that supply basic demographic and health information as well as global positioning. You will be able to get in your car and follow directions to your wandering dog. Not only that, but speeding cars will be alerted to slow down when a dog sporting a chip nears a road. Your car computer will ring out "Dog approaching twenty feet."

Dog School

Don't want your dog staying at home alone? Send him to dog school. Yes, during the workday, your dog can play in a structured environment optimized to increase his learning, with small classes taught by professional trainers. The idea of a dog understanding 5 words will be revolutionized by dog school graduates with 100-word vocabularies. Wait lists will be long and tuition steep. Dog school will be open late to accommodate late work hours, travel, and dinner out. Don't forget to order a class photograph! If you find yourself staying at home because of the dog, head into the city and drop the dog off at an evening facility while you enjoy a dinner in town. No need to rush home. A professional will take care of your dog while you're out.

Flying in Style

Planning a European vacation? Don't forget the dog. Pet transport services for medium- and large-breed dogs will improve so dogs can fly in style. No longer relegated to the noisy cargo bin, dogs and owners will be able to travel in a reserved seating/lounging area—first-class cabin, of course. Potty issues on long flights will need some special engineering, but there's hope for improvement. Another option will be to first—class express mail your dog. Private mail companies will construct roomy, dog-friendly, ventilated, temperature-controlled pens for high-in-the-sky comfort between major international airports.

Spa Homes to Come

Already, you can customize your home to make it the ultimate pooch pad. New construction will offer dog-owner packages with built-in doghouses, luxury outdoor kennels to match the main house, electronic dog doors, doggy cam surveillance systems (so you can see your dog from work), electric perimeter fencing, point-of-use plumbing at floor level and self-serve water pedals (let Fido fill his own water bowl), and, of course, the indoor or outdoor dog agility gym (treadmill not included). Custom dog baths will make home grooming easier by adding hand-held nozzles spraying both shampoo and water, with an added bonus of clog-proof plumbing. Expect to see ventilation systems built to ultrafilter pet hair and dander to reduce allergies. New housing developments will be preplanned with sidewalks and a dog park. Cities and towns will continue to respond to residents' demands for off-leash green space, swimming, and play areas. House cleaning services will expand to include grooming, dog massage, dog linen changes, yard, food- and water-bowl cleaning, and interior car servicing to keep your dog's carriage mud- and fur-free.

Luxury Dog Homes

La Petite Maison can design and construct Fido's dream house. For two-in-one use, a dream doghouse can also double as a dream playhouse for a child. Your dog may just attend the play tea party if he is enticed with high-tea shortbreads.

Prepackaged Fresh Meals

Looking for your dog's next meal? Well, if it wasn't delivered straight to your door, you can pick it up fresh at the grocery store. Nutritionally balanced, each prepackaged fresh meal will include a serving of raw meat, vegetable, fruit, grain, and dairy. Meals will be organic to protect your dog from hormones and pesticides. Pick a meal perfect for your dog's nutritional requirements: low fat, high protein, low calorie. When will some famous weight-loss author start selling dog food? Better yet, when can we start sending our dogs to fat-dog camps? Dog restaurants are cropping up, though they may not have arrived in your town yet. When they do, keep the menu in your car for quick take-out orders. Eat in for the ambiance.

Hospital Services for Your Dog

Veterinary services will expand to include dog spa offerings, acupressure and acupuncture, hydrotherapy, and, of course, expensive dog food. Oh, wait, I think veterinarians are already selling expensive dog food. You will also be able to visit the doggy psychiatrist to address emotional problems during your dog's checkup. Both dogs and owners will live longer, so medical animal services will continue to be cutting-edge, providing modern cancer and orthopedic treatments. Veterinarians will incorporate and expand on a variety of services such as spa, boarding, grooming, and supplies. No visit to the veterinarian will be complete without a cleaning by the dental hygienist.

Dog Spa-ahhhhs

Equipped to rival any human salon, dog spas of the future will make owners swoon with envy. Luxurious, thick-carpeted lobbies will be staffed by attentive receptionists who will escort your dog to his pampering sessions. Service rooms will be draped in terry cloth and mood music. Aestheticians versed in coat treatments and relaxation techniques will apply the latest grooming products. Dogs will be able to take a refreshing postmassage swim in the spa pool. Light spa lunches will be available on request.

No-Guilt Vacations

Rated from one to five stars, dog hotels will have style and service to match their catchy names. Bottled dog-bowl water, daily room service, and resort activities will keep your pooch spoiled rotten. Missing your dog? Well, with four-legged friends to run after, he won't be missing you. Send him back year after year to a dog camp to visit his pals and escape to the country.

Conclusion

We pamper our dogs because our dogs deserve it. Devoted companions, dogs follow us in life to wherever we choose to lead them. Forgiving friends, they patiently wait for us to return home and follow us from room to room, ever present as we live our lives. Some things dogs like to do are purely dog (rolling in awful smells, for example). But they share so many of our interests, like relaxing, eating, and enjoying the beautiful outdoors. Wherever your life takes you, take your best friend. Think of his needs and doggy interests. Remember his coat when it's cold out. Give him quality food, lots of fresh water, and regular visits to the doctor. Learn to speak dog, and develop a common language with your buddy. Seek out interesting places. Get out and enjoy your world together. Create a safe haven that is clean, protected, and comforting. Groom and pamper your dog. Check his claws, ears, teeth, paws, and coat and look for any trouble areas that may need medical care. Practice an ounce of prevention to give your dog a long, healthy life with you. Love your dog. And most of all, don't forget that dogs need to go to the park and get a massage, a rub, or a big hug every day.

Resources

Dog Food

Artemis Pet Food Company
15204 Stagg Street
Van Nuys, CA 91405
818-786-3618
www.artemiscompany.com
Supplier of premium dog food

Natura Pet Products, Inc.
Innova, California Natural, Karma
P.O. Box 271
Santa Clara, CA 95052
408-261-0770
www.naturapet.com
www.karmaorganic.com
Premium and organic dog foods

Old Mother Hubbard/Wellness
Pet Foods
285 Mill Road
Chelmsford, MA 01824
800-225-0904
www.omhpet.com
Natural food for pets

The Wholistic Pet
P.O. Box 1107
Merrimack, NH 03054
888-452-7263
www.thewholisticpet.com
*Wholistic dog foods and
supplements*

Toys

Bohdi Toys
2554 Lincoln Boulevard, #369
Venice, CA 90291
310-822-3522
www.bodhitoys.com
Hip toys for dogs

Kyjen Company, Inc.
P.O. Box 793
Huntington Beach, CA 92648
714-841-1950
www.kyjen.com
*Great toys, games, and travel gear
for dogs*

Gear

Hogan Leather
15 Thomas Coles Lane
Wellfleet, MA 02667
508-349-7979
www.hoganleather.com
*Custom leather leashes and collars
for home and show*

Maine Cottage
Yarmouth, ME 04096
888-859-5522
www.mainecottage.com
Colorful home furnishings and
textiles

Orvis
Manchester, VT 05254
800-541-3541
www.orvis.com
Quality pet products, sporting
goods, home furnishings and more